AF654773

Tribal Culture, Health and Development

About the Editors

Kh. Narendra Singh is currently the Associate Professor and Head at the Department of Anthropology, Assam University, Diphu Campus, Diphu, Assam, India. Dr. Singh had his Master's and Ph.D. in Anthropology from University of Poona, Pune. Dr. Singh has vast experience in survey research and published several articles/research papers in national and international journals.

Binod C. Agrawal had his Ph.D. in Anthropology from University of Wisconsin (USA). Professor Agrawal is currently the Director General of TALEEM Research Foundation. Professor Agrawal was associated with Indian Space Research Organisation for more than two decades and he pioneered the India's first communication research Satellite Instructional Television Experiment (SITE). Professor Agrawal has published over dozen of books, several edited volumes and more than fifty articles/research papers in national and international Journals of repute.

Tribal Culture, Health and Development

A Study of North-East India

Editors
Kh. Narendra Singh
Binod C. Agrawal

CONCEPT PUBLISHING COMPANY PVT. LTD.
NEW DELHI-110059

© Editors

All rights reserved. No part of this work may be reproduced, stored, adapted, or transmitted in any form or by any means, electronic, mechanical, photocopying, micro-filming recording or otherwise, or translated in any language, without the prior written permission of the copyright owner and the publisher. The book is sold subject to the condition that it shall not, by way of trade or otherwise, be lent, resold, hired out, or otherwise circulated without the prior publisher's written consent in any form of binding or cover other than that in which it is published.

The views and opinions expressed in this book are author(s) own and the facts reported by him/her have been verified to the extent possible, and the publishers are not in any way liable for the same.

ISBN-13: 978-93-5125-218-4

First Published 2016

Published and Printed by

Concept Since 1974

Concept Publishing Company Pvt. Ltd.
A/15-16, Commercial Block, Mohan Garden,
New Delhi-110059 (INDIA)
Phones : 25351460, 25351794, *Fax* : 091-11-25357109
E-mail : publishing@conceptpub.com
Website: www.conceptpub.com

Editorial Office: H-13, Bali Nagar, New Delhi-110 015, India.

Tribal culture, health and development : a study of North-East India / editors, Kh. Narendra Singh, Binod C. Agrawal.
pages cm
Papers presented in a conference held at Diphu, Assam under the auspices of Assam University, Diphu Campus on October 20-21, 2012.
Includes bibliographical references and index.
ISBN 9789351252184

1. India, Northeastern—Social life and customs—Congresses. 2. Tribes—Medical care—India, Northeastern—Congresses. 3. India, Northeastern—Scheduled tribes—Health and hygiene—Congresses. 4. Traditional medicine—India, Northeastern—Congresses. 5. Economic development—India, Northeastern—Congresses. I. Singh, Narendra Kh., editor. II. Agrawal, Binod C., editor.

DS483.4.T75 2016 DDC 306.09541 23

Preface

The Scheduled Tribes development is a serious proposition and it has a bearing with socio-cultural change and realities, practical and variable solution. Scheduled Tribes communities still represents the lowest stratum of the development in the country because the benefits of anti-poverty scheme have not reached to them. There is a general agreement that the health situation of the Indian tribal population is poor, and there is high incidence of anemia among the Scheduled Tribe mothers and children due to lack of necessary nutritional intake.

North East India is the homeland of a large number of ethnic groups who came from different directions at different historical times. The diverse Mongoloid groups in course of time settled down in different habitats and ecological settings of the north-eastern region crystallized into distinct entities which are referred to as Scheduled Tribes today (Bhagabati, 1988). These groups belong to different ethnic communities, speak different dialects and have varied cultural traditions. There are approximately 145 Scheduled Tribes communities living in North East India constituting around 12 per cent of the total Scheduled Tribes population of India and 26 per cent of the total population of North East India. More than eighty per cent of the Scheduled Tribes population are residing in rural areas of the region. Despite its rich natural endowment, the region suffers from economic stagnation.

The present volume offers an overview of the culture, health and development of the Scheduled Tribe communities of North East.

There are altogether twelve chapters in this volume containing variety of issues. Four chapters are on culture of North East India, five chapters on health and nutritional problems and other three chapters on development aspects of the region.

Dr. Binod C. Agrawal's article on "Culture, Communication and Health in North East Region: An Anthropological Perspective" laid stress on the analysis of the conflict situations among various social groups who were mistakenly referred to as tribes by British colonial imperialists and later were re-designated as Scheduled Tribes in the Independent India by the framers of the Constitution. Dr Agrawal also described the impact of digital communication revolution in the lives of relatively protected inhabitants of North East region from external influences. He also expressed about the cultural implication of digital communication as modern youth are seen attractive to Western culture due to access to internet facilities and other forms of media. Dr. Agrawal also examined health status of the people of North East region especially HIV/AIDS infection, its protection, prevention and spread.

In his article "Traditional Art and Architecture of Dwelling House: A Descriptive Study", Mr. Haokip draws a historical analysis of the dwelling house of the Kuki society of North East India. He emphasized on the rituals performed during the selection procedure of village, village-gate and house site, preparation of materials, architectural structure, pattern and decoration of a house were some of the artifact characteristics of typical Kuki house. Mr. Haokip also mentioned that modernization, lack of preservation, disrespect of traditional properties and ethnic cleansing in the region may be some of the reasons, why traditional typical house are on the verge of extinction.

Dr. Narendra Singh in his article "Manipuri dance: The beautiful exponent of Manipuri Culture" emphasised on dance and culture narrated the various dance forms and their importance in Manipuri culture. Dr. Singh emphasised that for Manipuris, dance is not just a form of art, but a way of life. Intensely devotional in mood, the Manipuri dances are a part of the daily life of the Manipuri people. Such beautiful dance forms need to be made to preserve the essence and authenticity.

Dr. Ansari in his paper "History, Society and Culture of Medieval Assam in *Fat-he Ibriya* of Shahabuddin Talish" described about Assam and Cooch Behar during second half of the seventeenth century.

In the paper "Indigenous Healthcare Practices among the Karbis of Assam: A study on the role of women" Reena Terangpi and co-authors discussed on the traditional medicine is prevalent among the Karbis of Assam, as first line of primary healthcare. The authors emphasised for proper documentation and identification of active principles of traditional medicines needs to be expedited owing to current trend of loss of biodiversity and before the knowledge-holders die.

The paper entitled "Health of Pre-adolescent Sonowal Kacharis of Dibrugarh district, Assam" Dr. Jaswant Singh presented health and nutritional status of the Sonowal Kacharis aged 6 to 10 years determined by the indices height-for-age, weight-for-age and BMI. The findings revealed that the nutritional status of the Sonowal Kachari children, on average, moderate in comparison to some other North East Indian population.

In the paper "Ethnoichthyological Notes on the use of fish in Traditional Medicine among the Karbis of Assam", Valentina Teronpi and co-authors discussed the ethnomedicine and traditional healthcare practices of the Karbis is discussed. The authors observed that ichthyofauna is used as ethnomedicine to cure host of diseases like anaemia, muscular inflammation, analgesic etc. It is also used healthcare practices to cure mental depression like symptoms.

Atuwar Rahman in his paper "Health Care Practices in Tea-Estates in Cachar District of Assam: A Sociological Study" an studied the health care practices in tea estates of Cachar district; causes of poor health care practices in tea estates and implementation and impact of different health policy. The result shows the prevalence of traditional health care practices along with the modern health care practices.

In her paper "Effect of Several Anthropometric, Bio-social and Lifestyle Variables on the Bengali Hindu Female Breast Cancer Patients of the State of West Bengal, India: A Case-control Study" Pushpita Purkayastha made an attempt to report the prevalence of some anthropometric and lifestyle variables on the Bengali Hindu female breast cancer patients of West Bengal. The study revealed that statistically significant differences do not exist in most of the anthropometric variables of the groups. However, significant associations have been found between various lifestyle and bio-social variables with that of breast cancer.

Dr. Kh. Narendra Singh in his article "Sustainable Development and Tribal Youth of Assam" narrated the various measures have been taken by the State Government and NGOs by introducing programme for development of the Scheduled Tribe people that includes: educational programmes, economic programmes and health and sanitation programmes. Dr. Singh emphasised for income generation activities by providing special orientation trainings with a view to enhance their economic status of Scheduled Tribes youth. The welfare projects for the Scheduled Tribes need to be implemented with proper understanding of their culture incorporating the knowledge and experience of the Social, Cultural Anthropologists who have engaged in Scheduled Tribes' studies.

In the paper "Development Issues Related to the Tribes of North-East India" Borkiri Terang and Sangwaiso Teronpi emphasised on the Scheduled Tribes development issues include education, lack of infrastructure, poverty, extremist movements, literacy, health, tribal identity movements, unemployment, displacement, and so on. The author emphasised that development in North East India must be treated with the utmost urgency and an all-round approach.

This paper will give a general assessment of various development issues and constraints to development among the Scheduled Tribes of North East India.

Mr. Haokip in his article "Poverty and Illiteracy in the Hill Districts of Manipur: Issues and Concerns" studies the poverty situations and the high rate of illiteracy prevailing in the villages in the interior areas of Manipur. The article also intends to point out the factors responsible for the adverse situations in the hills which may have a general bearing on most hill districts of the Northeastern India.

We are glad to present this volume to the readers and like to record our appreciation and thanks to all the contributors who assisted in the effort.

May 5, 2015

Kh. Narendra Singh
Binod C. Agrawal

Acknowledgements

The book emerged out of a conference held at Diphu, Assam under the auspices of Assam University, Diphu campus, on October 20-21, 2012. We gratefully acknowledge the support provided by Vice Chancellor Professor Somnath Dasgupta, faculty staff and organizing committee of the conference. We also acknowledge the participants and paper presenters who came all the way to Diphu for attending the conference. Last but not the least we are grateful to the faculty of Department of Anthropology and the students to help, manage the conference. Hope this book will be useful to the readers to provide fresh insight of several problems including health.

Kh. Narendra Singh
Binod C. Agrawal

Contents

Contributors

A.K. Tamuli, Associate Professor & Head, Department of Life Science & Bioinformatics, Assam University, Diphu Campus, Diphu-782 462, Assam

Atuwar Rahman, Research Scholar, Assam University, Silchar-11, E-mail: arrahmanassam@gmail.com

Binod C. Agrawal, Director General TALEEM Research Foundation, Ahmedabad-380 058 Email: binodcagrawal@gmail.com

Borkiri Terang, Assistant Professor, Department of Political Science, Diphu Government College, Diphu-782 460, Assam, E-mail: borkiri@gmail.com

Hemphi Terangpi, Department of Botany, Diphu Government College, Diphu, Karbi Anglong, Assam.

Jaswant Singh, Assistant Professor, Department of Anthropology, Dibru College, Dibrugarh-786 003, Assam.

Kh. Narendra Singh, Associate Professor & Head, Department of Anthropology, Assam University: Diphu Campus, Diphu-782 462, Assam. Email: kh.singh@rediffmail.com

Ngamkholen Haokip, Research Scholar, Department of Visual Art, Assam University; Silchar, Email: pupatimes@yahoo.com

Ni-et Teronpi, Department of Botany, Diphu Government College, Diphu, Karbi Anglong, Assam.

Pushpita Purkayastha, Junior Research Fellow, Anthropological Survey of India, NERC, Shillong.

Reena Terangpi, Assistant Professor, Department of Botany, Diphu Government College, Diphu, Karbi Anglong, Assam.

Robindra Teron, Assistant Professor, Department of Life Science & Bioinformatics, Assam University: Diphu Campus, Diphu-782 462, Assam. Email: robin.teron@gmail.com

Sangwaiso Teronpi, Assistant Professor, Department of Political Science, Diphu Government College, Diphu-782 460, Assam.

E-mail: sangwaisoteronpi@gmail.com

T.H. Ansari, Assistant Professor, Department of History, Assam University: Diphu Campus, Diphu-782 462, Assam.

Thenkhogin Haokip, Research Scholar, Department of Education, Assam University, Silchar-788 011, E-mail: ginneo@rediffmail.com

Valentina Teronpi, Research Scholar, Department of Life Science & Bioinformatics, Assam University: Diphu Campus, Diphu-782 462, Assam Email: valentina.teronpi@gmail.com

SECTION 1 : CULTURE OF NORTH EAST INDIA

1
Culture, Communication and Health in North East Region

An Anthropological Perspective

Binod C. Agrawal

Introduction

I think there is a need for deeper understanding of some of the historical, geo-political and economic factors that have devastated and kept the North East region in perpetual conflict, tension and human misery. These factors must be analysed and understood dispassionately to solve the tribulations to move forward. My modest attempt today would be to touch upon three interlinked issues that may throw some answers for the development and well-being of inhabitants of North East region. I will attempt:

1. To revisit the colonial history for trying to understand and analyse the conflicts among various social groups who were mistakenly referred to as tribes by British colonial imperialists and later were redesignated as Scheduled Tribes in the independent India by the framers of the Constitution;
2. To briefly describe the impact of digital communication revolution in the lives of relatively protected inhabitants of North East region from external influences who leaped frog appropriate development of infrastructure, transport

connectivity and industrial revolution. The bombshell of digital communication revolution confronted while embracing Christianity that led to become world citizens; and

3. To examine how has these two developments affected health of North East region especially HIV/AIDS infection, its protection, prevention and spread.

Colonial Past

In 1921, J.H. Hutton, long time British civil servant compiled his observations on Sema Naga and published a book in 1922. At that time, there was no State of Nagaland. Hutton (1922) also provided in his monograph a map which indicated the territory of Sema Naga.

Hutton in the 2nd edition of '*The Sema Nagas*' (1968) observed:

> Since, the first edition of this [The Sema Nagas] volume was published in1922, the Sema Naga tribe has undergone a very complete change. The account given was compiled mostly between the years 1915 and 1920, and whereas today the whole tribe forms part of Nagaland and is almost, if not entirely, Christian, of the American Baptist persuasion, it was then almost entirely pagan, and that portion of it living east of the Tizu river was unadministered and only interfered with by British officials when it made the error of collecting a head from some members of an administered and revenue paying village asked for the services of the Deputy Commissioner at Kohima, or the Subdivisional Officer of Mokokchung, as a mediator to settle some dispute with another village... The Semas east of Tizu were continually at war with their neighbours to the east, and also from time to time with one another. The migratory expansion of the tribe at the expense of less warlike

> neighbours had not yet entirely ceased, and traditions of origin were still recent enough to make it possible to plot the movements of the tribe from the Manipur state northwards and thence eastwards...Most of all this is now part of the pagan past and likely to be forgotten in the breach of continuity which conversion to Christianity has brought about. [Hutton 1968: Preface]

The observations of Hutton (1968) about Sema Naga territory in the present day political map of India does not conform to Nagaland. Same holds true for other States like Arunachal Pradesh, Assam, Manipur, Meghalaya, Mizoram, Nagaland, Sikkim and Tripura. These anomalies continue to be caused of conflict and tension in whole of North East region.

Recent Bodo-Muslim conflict in Assam and aftermath in other parts of India can be historically placed to the annexation of Assam by British almost two centuries ago. Upadhyaya (2012) reported "Various historical developments since the annexation of Assam by the British in 1826 suggests that the protracted demographic invasion from erstwhile eastern Bengal to Assam has been one of the major sources of ethnic bitterness and tension in the region. The ongoing Bodo-Muslim clash is an offshoot of this bitterness." One can cite a large number of such unfortunate incidences of continuous conflict; confrontation and political upheaval in North East region and elsewhere after India's independence in 1947 (also *see* Routray, 2008).

A large part of India lived in the diverse mosaic of civilizations for over five millennia full of continuous crisis and conflicts accentuated by hoard of immigrants from Central Asia, West Asia and North and South-East Asia. Several external invasions have generated certain degree of acceptance of diversity and tolerance for alien religions and cultures within the subcontinent. At the same time it continuously provoked and manifested sublime intolerance and latent aggressions against one and each other. Recorded history of about two hundred years has documented several such conflicts among family, community and territory.

Even after partition of British India, on the basis of religion, in 1947, and further partition of Bangladesh and Pakistan in 1971, the process of clashes are unabated.

The post-colonial North East region and for that matter, the whole of India has been experiencing the impact of redrawing of village, district, state and political boundaries in the last sixty-five years for expediency and to fulfil the aspirations of diverse linguistic and social groups. The same has been felt most in North East region. In the process, social identities have been fractured, divided and subverted creating further apprehensions of loss of self-esteem, freedom and loyalties. North East region has had experienced severe stress and strain in the process compared to other parts of India accentuated by claims and counter-claims within and from outside. In 2003, Fernandes (2003:1) reported "Assam is in news again for all wrong reasons and usual causes of ULFA and other militant outfits being behind the unrest…". Among many factors and deeper causes of unrest include decades of neglect and economic forces and devaluation of culture (Fernandes, 2003:1). Gradual loss of job in the tea gardens, replacement of local workers by migrant cheap labour led to serious conflicts are other associated regions. "…In recent years there have been many conflicts for land and forests that have resulted in massacres. Be it the Naga-Kuki conflict in Manipur, the Bodo-Santhal and Dimasa-Hmar tension in Assam or the Tripura tribal demand(s) for a homeland all have their origin in competition for land." (Fernandes, 2003:2).

My intension in highlighting the loss of human lives due to clashes and conflicts in North East region is to emphasize the omnipresent, perennial and continuing crisis and conflict across large part of India especially after 1947. As an anthropologist, I take the view of clash and conflict as a socio-political process emanating out of culture contact, conflict and change in the subcontinent expressed in political and economic aspirations to have money, power and territorial control among different linguistic and religious groups. The process has been further compounded in the multilingual, multi-religious civilization having high degree of continuing and uninterrupted social differentiation in different parts of India.

Hence, it is tentatively concluded that continuous clash and conflict has been inherent in the Indian civilization which has been magnified in the democratic political system of India. Individual aspirations and vested interest of international community has added fuel in the fire on ongoing basis.

Digital Communication Revolution in North East Region

I like to go back in mid-eighties of twentieth century to start discussion on digital communication revolution in North East region. BBC computer was introduced in the higher secondary schools of North East region, as a part of Computer Literacy and School Studies (CLASS) project during 1984-85 (*See* Agrawal, 1990). At this juncture in history, North East region experienced and started enjoying video viewing. CLASS project was evaluated by A.C. Bhagabati (*See* Bhagabati, Annada, C. and Meenakshi Das, 1986, and also *see* Agrawal, 1990). The video penetration study was carried out by A.C. Sinha (*See* A.C. Sinha, 1986, also *see* Agrawal, 1989). However, computer in higher education for research, teaching and administration remained limited in early nineties (*See* Achuthan, Agrawal, Shah, Soni and Thakore, 1993).

The situation today is drastically different. Computer technology use has spread across North East region at all levels of education and administration. However, there is no conclusive evidence to demonstrate that computer has helped to equalize the learning opportunities or has reduced the information gap between poor and rich (Agrawal, 2003).

On the other hand in spite of government control, video libraries, video cassette recorders and cable television appeared in North East region very rapidly adopting new technologies leading to disappearance of video libraries. The real impetus for video use came from Hindi and English films in variety of ways and reached in the remotest part of North East region. Today, satellite television has invaded majority of homes of North East region where viewers are watching language based regional telecast, national and international, private and public service telecast from across the world.

I strongly believe that there is a need for contextual evaluation to assess differential computer response of various regions so as computer can be meaningfully used for the development of North East region. Available data and observations indicated rapid expansion of computer and digital information technology whether desktop or laptop in business, banking, education, industry, government and affluent homes though backup support continues to mark efficient information technology use.

The rapid changes and unprecedented expansion that have connected through two-way communication to the North East region with the rest of world is telecommunications and internet access. Mobile phones can be seen in every adult hand anywhere and everywhere in North East region. The globe has become time and distance neutral. Private sector has played an important role in the expansion of mobile telephony.

In the post-economic liberalization phase of 1992, North East region has experienced truly digital communication revolution like rest of India by skipping landline phones and literacy and language barriers. It must be noted that the impact of digital communication revolution has been profound. Telecommunications whether mobile telephone, i-pad, i-phone and Internet are all being used for continuous communication.

Digital communication revolution continues to help communities, individual tribes, and states of North East region to assert for self-identity, autonomy and freedom of expression. There has been all-round impact of digital communication revolution including health care. In the remaining part of the presentation, I shall try to analyse and discuss HIV/AIDS awareness, its spread and methods of control, if any, with the help of digital communication revolution.

Health in Northeast Region

In amidst of continuous conflict, tension and strife in one form or the other, North East region has suffered apart from other things, decline in population growth in last decade of 2001-2011. Population growth in States of Arunachal Pradesh, Meghalaya and Mizoram could be attributed to labour migration from other parts of India and from neighbouring countries. Other factor

Table 1.1: Population Growth in North East Region between 2001 and 2011

		Census 2011			*2001*
State		*Total*	*Urban*	*Rural*	
Assam	Persons	31,169,272	4,388,756	26,780,516	26,655,528
	Males	15,954,927	2,265,188	13,689,739	13,777,037
	Females	15,214,345	2,123,568	13,090,777	12,878,491
	Population Growth	16.93%			18.85%
Tripura	Persons	3,671,032	960,981	2,710,051	3,199,203
	Males	1,871,867	486,362	1,385,505	1,642,225
	Females	1,799,165	474,619	1,324,546	1,556,978
	Population Growth	14.75%			15.74%
Meghalaya	Persons	2,964,007	595,036	2,368,971	2,318,822
	Males	1,492,668	297,911	1,194,757	1,176,087
	Females	1,471,339	297,125	1,174,214	1,142,735
	Population Growth	27.82%			29.94%
Manipur	Persons	2,721,756	822,132	1,899,624	2,293,896
	Males	1,369,764	403,500	966,264	1,161,952
	Females	1,351,992	418,632	933,360	1,131,944
	Population Growth	18.65%			30.02%
Nagaland	Persons	1,980,602	573,741	1,406,861	1,990,036
	Males	1,025,707	301,112	724,595	1,047,141
	Females	954,895	272,629	682,266	942,895
	Population Growth	-0.47%			64.41%
Arunachal Pradesh	Persons	1,382,611	313,446	1,069,165	1,097,968
	Males	720,232	165,928	554,304	579,941
	Females	662,379	147,518	514,861	518,027
	Population Growth	25.92%			26.21%
Mizoram	Persons	1,091,014	561,977	529,037	888,573
	Males	552,339	281,020	271,319	459,109
	Females	538,675	280,957	257,718	429,464
	Population Growth	22.78%			29.18%
Sikkim	Persons	607,688	151,726	455,962	540,851
	Males	321,661	79,539	242,122	288,484
	Females	286,027	72,187	213,840	252,367
	Population Growth	12.36%			32.98%

Source: http://www.census2011.co.in/states.php.

could be inter-tribal competition to boost population in Meghalaya among Garo, Khasi and Jaintiya though they have also shown decennial marginal decline from 29.94 per cent in 2001 to 27.82 per cent in 2011. On the whole, the decennial population growth showed decline in all States and minus growth in Mizoram (*See* Table 1.1). Health care of HIV/AIDS in North East region must be analysed while keeping the population decline trends in view.

HIV/AIDS Scenario in North East Region

In the North East region "Manipur is one of the six high prevalence states in India with HIV prevalence rate among pregnant women attending ANC being 1.4 per cent (Sentinel Surveillance 2006). Manipur with hardly 0.2 per cent of India's population is contributing nearly 8 per cent of India's total HIV positive cases. More and more interior and hill areas are affected and yet to be covered" (Roy, 2012: 2). Other populations including are equally susceptible and exposed to HIV/AIDS infection.

Three major ways of HIV spread—include sexual contact, blood transfusion, blood products and stained needles and syringes and vertical transmission—through mother to foetus. The principal mode of HIV transmission in North East region is primarily heterosexual contact. Furthermore, there is growing evidence that presence of a sexually transmitted disease (STD) has greatly affected acquisition and transmission of HIV infection in the region.

Information and education are critical inputs to be given to reduce incidence of HIV/AIDS infection through communication. State AIDS control societies have been formed, to evolve area-specific communication strategies to control HIV/AIDS. North East region presents multicultural ecologies, in which interpersonal and community relationships influence health and illness, including HIV/AIDS. Hence, community (tribe) specific media campaigns must engage individuals within their cultural environments.

Today Nagaland has a Naga identity having less than 2 million population. Nagaland touches the international border of Myanmar. Today Ao, Chang, Chakesang, Sangtam, Konyak, Angami, Sema and Lotha in spite of linguistic and cultural diversity have common religion of Christianity embraced little over a century ago. The meta analysis in Nagaland of sexually active women in the age group of 15-44 and their husbands (men) indicated high level of awareness of HIV/AIDS and RTI/STI though the awareness is higher among men as compared to women (*See* Table 1.2). It is important point to be made is that out of five, four men and women in Nagaland were aware of HIV/AIDS, which could be amongst the highest in the country (82.0 per cent women and 85.3 per cent men) though RTI/STI awareness level was below 50 per cent (*See* Table 1.2). Over 80 per cent HIV/AIDS awareness in Nagaland can be attributed to digital communication revolution and education.

Table 1.2: Awareness of HIV/AIDS and RTI/STI

Awareness level	*Nagaland*
Awareness of HIV/AIDS	
Women	82.0
Men	85.3
Total	83.6
Awareness of RTI/STI	
Women	43.0
Men	48.8
Total	45.8

Source: National Family Health Survey (NFHS-3) 2005-06.

Further comparative analysis of Assam, Meghalaya and Nagaland indicated that Nagaland women had very high degree of information about HIV/AIDS (80.3%) compared to Meghalaya (55.0%) and Assam (37.2%) (*see* Table 1.3). Religion and education might have contributed for such a differential level of HIV/AIDS information. Due to digital communication revolution in spite of relative geographical isolation, Nagaland Christian women had heard of HIV/AIDS most and were better informed as compared to Hindu and Christian women of Assam to the extent rural illiterate Hindu women seemed to be in "high risk" HIV/AIDS category due to lack of awareness (Table 1.3).

Table 1.3: Percentage Distribution of Respondents Heard of HIV/AIDS by State, Age, Education and Religion

	Assam			*Meghalaya*			*Nagaland*		
	Heard	*Not Heard*	*Total*	*Heard*	*Not Heard*	*Total*	*Heard*	*Not Heard*	*Total*
Age									
15-19	30.4	69.6	56	35.0	65.0	60	88.9	11.1	54
20-29	47.1	52.9	1134	61.8	38.2	1237	80.6	19.4	1103
30-39	32.4	67.6	1176	53.9	46.1	947	82.9	17.1	1061
40-44	27.8	72.2	550	43.0	57.0	507	73.5	26.5	536
Education									
Illiterate	8.3	91.7	1345	27.0	73.0	855	43.3	56.7	598
1-5 Class	34.1	65.9	419	59.0	41.0	819	83.6	16.4	207
6-9 Class	61.1	38.9	612	69.4	30.6	779	88.8	11.2	780
10+ Class	84.4	15.6	540	86.9	13.1	298	92.9	7.1	1169
Religion									
Christian	25.3	74.7	150	54.9	45.1	2588	80.3	19.7	2731
Hindu	37.9	62.1	2729	37.8	62.2	45	50.0	50.0	6
Others*	37.8	62.2	37	63.6	36.4	118	88.2	11.8	17
Total	1085 (37.2)	1831 (62.8)	2916 (100)	1514 (55.0)	1237 (45.0)	2751 (100)	2211 (80.3)	543 (19.7)	2754 (100)

* Others include Muslim, Buddhist, Sikh and others.
Source: National Family Health Survey (NFHS-3) 2005-06.

Inter-state differences observed in the degree of HIV/AIDS awareness call for separate communication approach and fresh research for all States for designing any communication strategy. Education seems to be the single most important determinant in creating awareness about HIV/AIDS. It is suggested that communication strategies must be designed keeping in view that women by and large in North East region play a prominent role in domestic and community activities. Also women encounter sexual experiences early in their lives. Women should be encouraged to persuade their men folks to use condom for safe sex and sex denial to men without condom use should be advocated. Interpersonal communication continued to be a prime mode of sharing and exchanging views of HIV/AIDS. Hence, it is suggested that apart from electronic and print media, interpersonal communication and locally popular means of communication must form an integral part of HIV/AIDS strategy. Efforts should be made to utilize health workers including doctors in creating awareness of HIV/AIDS who are currently least involved in promoting health care.

References

Achuthan, Sarla, Agrawal, Binod C., Shah, Vimal P., Soni, R.P. and Thakore, S.R. (1993), *Computer Technology for Higher Education,* Volume II, *The Indian Experience*. New Delhi: Concept Publishing Company.

Agrawal, Binod C. (2003), Structural Predicaments and Digital Divide: How Real in South Asia? In *Globalization and Challenges for Education*; compiled by Yazali Josephine; pp. 492-499. New Delhi: Shipra Publications.

———, (Assisted by Madhvi Joshi), (1990), *Pedagogy of Computer Literacy: An Indian Experience*, New Delhi: Concept Publishing Company.

Bhagabati, Ananda C. and Das, Meenakshi, (1986), *Evaluation of Computer Literacy and Studies in Schools (CLASS) in Guwahati*, unpublished Project Report sponsored by DECU, ISRO, Ahmedabad.

Fernandes, Walter, (2003), Why is Assam Burning?. *The Hindu*, December 8, 2003.

Hutton, J.H. (1922, 1968), *The Sema Nagaso*, Bombay, London: Oxford University Press (Second Edition).

Roy, Eshas (2012), *Pilot Loan Scheme for HIV-patients in Manipur,* http://www.indianexpress.com/news/pilot-loan-scheme-for-hivpatients-in-manipur/916797/

Routray, Bidhu Prasad (2008), *Violence in Assam Battle for the Bodo Heartland*. Institute of Peace and Conflict Studies, New Delhi, No. 85, October 2008.

Sinha, A.C., (1986), *Video Penetration in Northeast India*. Shillong: North Eastern Hill University (unpublished Report Sponsored by DECU, ISRO, Ahmedabad).

Upadhaya, R., (2012), *Bodo-Muslim Conflict in Assam–Historical Roots*. South Asia Analysis Group. Paper no. 5178, 23-Aug-2012. http://www.southasiaanalysis.org/%5Cpapers52%5Cpaper5178.html

2
Traditional Art and Architecture of Dwelling House

A Descriptive Study

Ngamkholen Haokip

Introduction

The word dwelling and house defined by the Illustrated Oxford Dictionary is "Dwelling" as "a house or other place where someone live" and "House" as "a building for people to live". Another Cambridge School Dictionary defined "House" as "a building where people live, usually one family or group". From the above definitions, it came to light that, human beings lived in a dwelling house in group or family with the existence of their culture and state. Art and architecture of dwelling house also one of the cultural activities of human life. The dwelling house protects the occupants from heat, weather, and wild animals and even from the evil spirit and enemies in the olden days. There is highly necessity for living inside a formally constructed proper house. The technique, style of constructing a dwelling house is different according to the region, climate, and materials available and also depends on the concept of ethnic group.

About the Kukis

The term *Kuki* is claimed to have included all the *Chin-Kuki-*

Mizo ethnic group of people who trace their common origin from a mythological cave (Doungel, 2011), which was known as *Khul, Khur, Khurpui, Khurtu-bijin, Khor, Puk, Shinlung,* and *Chhinlung*. This claim of common origin validates the authenticity of the close affinity and inseparable blood relationship of the *Chin-Kuki-Mizo* ethnic stock who settle in India, Myanmar and Bangladesh. Thus, all the cave origin people were collectively known as *Kuki*s in the past. "...ethnically, culturally, linguistically, the Kuki-Chin-Mizo, they are one and the same people, having common ancestry, common history, and common customary practices" (Dena, 2011). According to Lt. Colonel J. Shakespeare the term "*Kuki*" has a definite meaning and includes *Aimol, Chothe, Chiru, Koireng, Kom, Purum, Anal, Lamkang, Maring, Mate, Moyon, Monsang, Gangte, Vaiphei, Simte, Paite, Thadou, Hmar, Zou* etc. (Shakespeare, 1975).

The Kukis believe in *Pathen* (God), who rules the Universe. They also believe in the existence of *Thilha* (evil spirit). Each *Kuki* village is held together by social, economic, religious and political bonds. The *Haosa* (Chief), who is the head of the Village administration, has the responsibility to provide security to his villagers socially, politically and economically, entirely guided by customs and conventions. And his (Chief) *Semang-Pachong's* (Council Members) are the governing agents through which the chief administered the village. The customary law governs all criminal and civil cases. *Sa-Ai, Chang-Ai, Chonle-Han, Kut* etc. were the most popular festival of the *Kukis. Sa-Ai and Chang-Ai (Chon)* would only fulfil by the affluent and successful person in various ways which lifted them high in the society and also freed them of certain duties. It was everyman's dream to fulfil it. From 1909 CE, after the British conquered India, the Western Christian Missionaries convert them into Christian Religion.

The study of culture depends on the artifacts' left and found, like the study of Indus Valley Civilization culture depends on the artifacts excavated. The past history of culture, where there was no script to record, the remains of artifacts could be of great help to study all about that era. The study of material culture becomes one of the primary tools to know the tribes' inside-out. The traditional house of the *Kukis* was very typical and distinct from other ethnic's dwelling house.

General Structure of Dwelling House

The *Kukis* mostly built their village on the side of a hill. And, their house rests some 3 feet off the ground, on the up-hill side it is perhaps 15 and 20 feet off the ground and supported by long posts on the down-hill side (Tuck, 1987). Bertram S. Carey and H.N. Tuck's statement about this is only for the village house built on the hill side. There were also some *Kuki* village built on plain area or some houses built on the plain. The area of the house built may be on the plain or the hill side, but, all are in one-storied pattern and structure, built of plank, with a thatch roof, and 20 feet high by 50 to 200 feet long and some 30 feet broad, according to the position and affluence of the owner (Tuck, 1987).

Though there was no restriction, a house faces the East generally. There is hardly any variation in the house types. The variations of the house depend on the economic condition of the household. Generally, traditional dwelling house is a continuous roomy structure without any partition and window. The house is built off the ground in one-storey, underneath is the pig and cattle pen. A long platform in the front of the house has front verandah. In the hill side, the house structure is measured around three feet above the ground on the up-hill side, 15 and 20 feet above the ground on the down-hill side. In plain side, the floor of a house is just three to five feet above the ground level. The thatch of the house is often four or six feet long; it is laid on a foot thick and is often not removed when the house requires re-thatching, the new thatch being piled on over the old. In front of the house a yard quite flat levelling is cut out of the side of the hill.

Mutua Bhadur gives a short and clear description (skeletal structure) of typical *Kuki* house which was built in his owned museum at Andro, 18 km form Imphal. By seeing this, one can study the complete traditional house of the *Kukis*. Mutua Bhadur has done great works not only in this Museum, but also published a number of books on Art and Material Culture of Manipur. His statement "....typical house of *Kuki* tribes of Manipur, who are inhabited in the districts of Churachandpur and Sadar Hills, is known as *Malai Kuki* Inn (Bhadur, 2006). Here, *"Malai Kuki Inn"* literally means Traditional Kuki House. The *Kukis* are not only inhabited in the districts of Churachandpur and Sadar Hills, but they are also found in all other Hill Districts of Manipur and small number in Valley District. This type of traditional *Kuki* house is also found in areas where the *Kukis* are. But, today, due to Naga-Kuki ethnic clashed in 1990s and modernization has changed the typical *Kuki* house very less traditional house could be found.

To build a village and to construct a house, the *Kukis* performed a ritual for selection of village and house location. Ncy Doungel, in her book "Puchon Pachon" (customary practices of the *Thadou-Kukis*) give the details how village, village-gate and house sites are chosen in the tradition of ritual performance. The ritual to choose the village site is performed by "Egg". The egg is holed in the end, and kept on three stick posted in triangular position like *"lungthu"* a three post erected for cooking (Doungel, 2009).

According to the result of ritual, they select the site for village. If the site was selected for village, the priest will go and offer/ alter a mature Cock in the site. After selecting the village site, selection of village-gate site is also done in the process of ritual performance. To select the village-gate site, *"Ai"* (a kind of rhizome which has medicinal value) is used (Haokip, 2012). A piece of *Ai* is divided into two by the use of dao in the edge of a podhole made nearby. If the two pieces of *Ai* faced downside, then they burried the two pieces of *Ai* and animal heads are hang-out in the place. In the meantime, they also erected a stone. The erection of stone in village-gate is also performed in a ritual way (Doungel, 2009). So, all the *Kuki* villages have village-gate called *"Khomol* or *Dongkot"* with big stones erected at the site. Most of the *Kuki* villages were fenced with split logs for secutity purposes (Haokip H. 2009).

Like the village site and village-gate site are selected, a ritual is also performed to select the site for constructing a dwelling house. To select the site for constrution a space is clean-up and *"Anchang"* (Rice) is kept there for a night. If all the rice placed at the same place were not disturbed, they choose that very site for construction. And then after that only they started the necessary works for construction (Doungel, 2009).

Some of the main parts of a house are: *Sambuh* (Verandah), *Kotpi* (Main door), *Shutkhom* (Main pillar), *Khangphei* (Dormitory), *Lhongpeh* (Floor), *Kem* (Stage/Platform), *Gaplheng* (Hanging Mat).

*Verandah (*Sambuh*)*

Generally, the houses have broad verandah in the front. The front verandah is divided into two equal parts. The upper part/floor verandah consist of platform *(Kem)* made of bamboo or wood and floor of the house. The roof of the house overhangs the front verandah, which is enclosed on three sides and decorated with the skulls of animals hung in rows on the wall. Above the lower verandah on the roof, a sacred traditionally ritual box called *Doi-Bom/Inn-doi* (sacred basket/the house-god) is hanged. Rice pounding mill with pounding stick and dry firewood's were also kept on the floor of the verandah.

The verandah was decorated with the skull of animals and birds hung in rows on the wall. All the heads of animals killed by the house owner were used as trophies and are exhibited there. Anyone wishing to be informed of the class of game which found in any particular neighbourhood has only to pay a visit to the collection of skulls in the verandahs of the houses in the village (Tuck, 1987). The verandah is relatively small and used mainly by the women, while weaving and doing other household chores. The members of the household used to sit together, work or hold about and drink in the platform raised in front of the house. This also serves as a place where visitors are welcomed and during day time even crops are dried over it. All types of animals head/ skull killed by the house owner and sculpture are found here.

Sipra Sen's book "*The Tribes of Mizoram*" also states that, the trophies, skulls and horns of animals which they killed are proudly displayed by them in the main front portion of their house (Sen, 1992). Ethnographically, the Chins in Myanmar, *Kukis* in all parts of North-Eastern Indian States except Mizoram and Mizos or Lushais in Mizoram are of the same. According to the geographical area, materials available, influence of other ethnic groups their material cultures are different, but, structure and concepts are all the same. So, the statement of Sipra Sen "...they had no habituation to repair old and broken houses...and they had to leave that old house to be demolished...." In this case, the *Chin-Kuki* ethnic groups shifted the site of their houses for different reason. But, repairing of house and built a new one at the same site is also practice. And Ncy Doungel's statement "...they chose the location of the house from downhill side post/ pillar so as to avoid the practice of moving downhill side or forward and turning of the direction."

Another verandah was in the back side of the house, called *Kemcha* (small platform) with the door *Kotcha* (small door). The statement given by Bertram S. Carey and H.N. Tuck about the back verandah "....above the pig pen and is entered through a hole in the wall....referred to further on when the subject of gunpowder is dealt with...." Actually, the entrance through it was not a hole in the wall. It was a door small in size, called *kotcha*. *Kemcha* is used for urinal purpose by the whole family. So, after many decades of urinating at the same place, they extract gunpowder from that urine mixed clay. Because, it contains a chemical which may produced gunpowder. In this regard, scientific chemical test is required to proof. As back verandah was small in size, women folks preferred to use front verandah than back verandah.

***Main Door (*Kotpi)**

Main door of traditional *Kuki* house has two wooden planks. The making of main door needs a skilled man to carve. A big tree, about 30 inches diameter was divided into two pieces. Both the planks are hewed out from a large timber till the desire shaped and size was achieved. It is four to five feet in length and one and half to two feet in width and two to three inches thick. The bolt hinge for locking was hewned out called *"Kotbil"* on both sides. (Dongjakai, 2011) A cylindrical shape of rice pounding stick, locally called *"Suh"* measuring about four to five feet was inserted to the bolt hinge to lock the door. Everyone respect if the house door was closed, and there were no report of robbery or thieves. The main door of the house was called *Kotpi* and the other back door of the house was called *Kotcha* (Haokip, H., 2009). Though the Western styles of building were common to these days, the named *Kotpi* and *Kotcha* still exist in the modern houses too.

Main Pillar (*Shutkhom*)

There were many pillars in the structure of a house. *Shutkhom*—the main pillar in the middle of a house was bigger in size and double longer in length than the other pillars. Not only with textile design called *"changmaimu"* (cucumber seed) on it, and small branch to hang some man's equipment, (Haokip, S., 2012) has it also elongated textured like other pillars. It was the most important post in structural. The front side of the pillar is decorated with big animals head or skulls killed by the house owner, place of baskets or bags in the back. The post was erected in the middle of a house. Depending upon the size of a house, there was other two or four posts. The centre post of the main pillar is called *Shutlai-khom* (main and centre pillar), which also serves as the most important part in their custom and culture. It is a sacred ritual place or called Sacred Pillar. Ritual rites like *Saneng Het, jubel, Shutlai-Selpi* were performed traditionally. Different ceremonial, festive occasion and customary laws were also performed here. At the base of *Shutlai-khom* a rice-beer pot called *Jubel* was kept for a drink whenever they have customary related activities. Every customary issues verdict was taken with having the rice-beer.

*Dormitory (***Khangphei***)*

Khangphei was a long platform at a level little higher than that of the main floor, which was meant as a seating-cum-sleeping place (Haokip, H., 2009). Depending upon the availability of materials, it was made of either wooden planks or flattened bamboo matting (Haokip, M.A., 2009). *Khangphei* was the only sleeping place for the whole family. Even guest and youth also sleep at *Khangphei.* Holkhongam Haokip further states that, "the beds of the members of the family were placed on the both sides of the fire place where cooking was done." In olden days, there were no beds for the family members. *Khangphei* was the only sleeping place for both family members and guests. But, there was a place to sleep for family elders, family young girls, youths and guests. Big families have two dormitories, one for the youth and one for the married couples and family elders.

*Floor (***Lhongpeh***)*

Traditionally, the floor of a house was made of flattened bamboo splits or wooden plank. A bamboo called *Gopi* or *Gomi* of same size was used. A wooden plank hewn from a large timber by the used of *Heicha* (Axe) measuring two to four feet flat surface and 10-15 feet in length of solid trees are used. Bertram S. Carey and H.N. Tuck describe the floor of typical Kuki house as "....is made of pine planking ... and which are fitted together with skill and without the assistance of nails" (Tuck, 1987). The statement confined only to a particular area, so, the use of pine planking was mentioned. But, there were also some particular places where pine trees are not available. Depending on the availability of materials, they are very much interested in using the best material available in their location. They also have the knowledge and skill to fit them without the assistance of nails. Red wood, which resembles mahogany, was greatly used for the floors of the Chiefs' houses. Poor families used splits of bamboo locally called *Gopi* or *Gomi* on their floor. It has its own and traditional beauty. Other wooden planks used for floor are locally named *Uningthou, Leihao-thing, Chal-thing, Kha-thing, Banlhang-thing, Vong-thing, Khanglha-thing, Jangngou-thing, Chah-thing* etc. A tree is split into half by the use of small heavy-headed axe. Alun Haolai also described the floor of the traditional house in his book *"Kum Som-nga Kahinkho"* "….bamboo slice called *Gomi-Lhong*, measuring three cubits was the floor of a house…" (Haolai, 2002).

*Stage/Platform (*Kem)

A platform rose in front of the house was also one of the traditional architectural structures. It was built five to seven feet high above the ground level of bamboo or wood, depending on the materials available. "…platform from 20 to 100 feet in length occupies the whole length of the lower side and is supported by long posts like lower side of the house (Tuck, 1987). The members of the household used to sit together, work or hold about and drink on the platform. This also serves as a place where visitors were welcomed and during day time crops are dried over it. Young man's' used to sit here with their traditional musical instrument called *Goshem* under the moonlit at night and played for their love one's, who was inside the house.

Hanging Mat (Gaplheng)

Gaplheng is another striking art feature of the house. It is the hanging three tier bamboo mat just above the fire place or furnace. It was used to prepare and store dry food stuffs, dried meat, newly woven baskets, chili, maize etc. It serves as a shield against the sparks touching the roof. All this preserving and storing items made it more decorative. So, there is a saying *"A gaplheng a saphe kikhai lou"* (A hanging mat without dry meat) (Neijalhing, 2012). The literal meaning is that, the family without decorated hanging mat with dry meat is an idle or incomplete family, i.e. without hunter. Therefore, a family with dry meat on the hanging mat was suggestive of having a manly and honourable man in the family. The third tier of *Gaplheng* was the biggest in size and upper most layer of hanging mat. The second and middle one is used for storage of woven baskets small in size, and already dried food items. And the first tier was decorated with dry meat and newly bought food stuffs to dry. It was used for keeping big baskets, and other household items.

Conclusion

North East India, land of cultural diversity has its own beauty of traditional art and craft. Art comes to them instinctively. Every ethnic group has a unique way of living. The Kukis, one of the ethnic groups settled in Assam, Manipur, Mizoram and Nagaland also in Myanmar (Burma) and Bangladesh, have their own indigenous art and craft. The artifacts they used, the culture they practiced, the custom they followed are all sample tools to know their inside-out. They followed certain rules of art and craft guarded by their custom and culture. The tradition of living in a proper house was highly necessary for the Kukis too; to protect them from heat, weather, and wild animals and even from the evil spirit and enemies. To build the traditional dwelling house, they need a special planning, technique, skill and a creative mind. The houses of the *Kukis* were traditionally built on a slope and hilly site. They had only one storey underneath which there was space for cattle pen. The house was continuous room, without windows, and the front wall was decorated with animal heads and skulls.

After the coming of Christianity, *growing westernization influenced their traditional art forms.* Houses were then constructed with a decorated modern and better material like timber, bricks, stones and corrugated iron sheets for roofing. In addition, wooden furniture's like benches, tables, chairs have become a part and parcel of their modern ways of house materials. Hence, apart from the advent of Christianity, the social transformation of the *Kukis* occurred due to various factors. *Many of these artifacts are disappearing mainly due to lack of preservation and ethnic clash.* Also readily availability of a number of manufactured artifacts (especially plastic). *Collection and documentation of the materials, objects and the cultural artifacts is of primary importance today.* Each society is subjected to the changes brought about by the coming of Christianity and growing westernization. As such, it appears that there is *danger of negligence in one's own culture which may further lead to decay or extinction of the culture.*

References

1. Bhadur, M. (2006). *Guide Book: Mutua Museum Cultural Heritage Complex.* (L.B. Sharma, Ed.) Imphal: Mutua Museum.
2. Dongjakai, T. Kotpi. *Kotpi.* Tribal Museum, Churachandpur.
3. Doungel, N. (2009). *Puchon Pachon (Customary Practices of Thadou-Kuki)* (Second ed.). (N. Haokip, Trans.) Imphal: Tribal Research Institute, Imphal.
4. Haokip, H. (2009). *Christian Missionaries Among the Kukis: A Historical Study.* Imphal: Unpublished Thesis Submitted to Manipur University in partial fulfilment for the Award of the Degree of Doctor of Philosophy in History.
5. Haokip, M.A. (2009). *Chon: A Study on Chon, Greatest of the Thadou-Kuki Festival.* Imphal: Unpublished dissertation report submitted to the Department of Manipuri Dance, Manipur University in partial fulfilment of for the award of the degree of Master of Arts in Manipuri Dance.
6. Haokip, S. (2012, June 28). Village Elder and Craftsman. (N. Haokip, Interviewer, N. Haokip, Editor, & N. Haokip, Translator).
7. Haolai, A. (2002). *Kum Som-nga Kahinkho: Maap-gam le Manipur Lengte.* (N. Haokip, Trans.) Imphal: Author.
8. Neijalhing. (2012, March 21). Village Elder Woman. (N. Haokip, Interviewer, & N. Haokip, Translator) Churachandpur.
9. Sen, S. (1992). *The Tribes of Mizoram.* Delhi: Gian Publishing House.
10. Tuck, B.S. (1987). *The Chin Hills* (Vol. I). Delhi: Gian Publishing House.

3
Manipuri Dance
The Beautiful Exponent of Manipuri Culture

Kh. Narendra Singh

Introduction

In 1908, Hodson stated that the term "Meiteis" has been derived from mi = Man and Theie = Separate, as a combined appellate of Siamese "Tai" and Koch in Chinese "Moy". Chatterjee (1946) in his famous work "Kirata-Jana-Kirti" stated "The Meiteis or the Manipuris are the most advanced section of the Kuki-Chin people".

Singh (1973) describes the Meiteis as: "The people of Manipur in the valley, speaking the Manipuri language is known in the local language as the meiteis. Whenever references have been made about them in any book the word Manipuri has been used to denote the Meiteis.

"Although the general facial characteristics of the Manipuri are of the Mongolian type, there is a great diversity of feature among them, some of them showing a regularity approaching the Aryan type" (Dr. Brown).

Manipuris are mostly inhabited in Imphal valley and Jiribam in Manipur. A sizeable number of them are also lived in Cachar, Hailakandi, Karimganj, Sibsagar, Kamrup, Nagaon districts of Assam, Agartala, Bangladesh and Myanmar.

Manipuri language is a member of the Kuki-Chin group of

Manipuri language is a member of the Kuki-Chin group of the Tibeto-Burmese family of language. Manipuri is one of the popular languages of Northeastern India. Manipuri language has its own script which is found in old manuscripts.

Manipuri has a composite religion in which ancestor worship (ancestor of a clan is called '*Apoka*') and different Hindu cults have been welded together. There are seven clans among the Meiteis. These are: (1) The Ningthoujas (Mangang), (2) The Angoms, (3) The Khumans, (4) The Moirangs, (5) The Luwangs, (6) The Khaba-Nganbas and (7) The Sarang-Laisangthem (Chengloi). The time of King Chura Chand (1891-1941) showed a great achievement in Manipuri art and culture. The famous historical novel "Lavangalata" by Kh. Chaoba and romantic novel "Madhabi" by Dr. L. Kamal were written during the period.

Kaviguru Rabindranath Tagore was greatly impressed by Manipuri dance and he introduced Manipuri dance at Shanti Niketan as a subject. This led to the re-organization of Manipuri dance as one of the classical dance of India. Nat Sankirtan grew in excellence and "Pungcholom" also grew with popularity during the period.

Colonel McCullock describes the dress of the Manipuris on the following terms:

> "The men dress in same way they do in Hindustan, but as a people the Manipurees far surpass the people of the West in the cleanliness of their garments."

Dr. Brown, however, amplifies this account in the following passage, "the dress of the men does not differ materially from that of the Bengalese, and consists of the *dhoti*, a *Koorta*, a Shirt only occasionally worn, and shawl or sheet. The dress of women when of good quality is picturesque and pleasing. The women wear 'phanek' a piece of cloth made of cotton and silk, and the patters are stripes of various colours and width running across the materials over the phanek is worn a white sheet, in-a-phi which is folded in the usual native manner. A blanse or short or a light jacket is worn during winter season.

Regarding the ornaments worn by Meiteis Dr. Brown says that "the ornaments are ear-rings, necklace and bracelets; nose ornaments are limited to a small piece of gold wire in the side of each nostrils." The ear-rings worn by men and by the majority of the women are of plain gold. The bracelets and necklace are of chased and hammered patterns.

Manipuri Dance

Manipuri dance is the greatest exponent of Manipuri culture. It has been a welcome attribute of the Manipuri culture that it never becomes static in form but adapted itself to the variation of time and space. Culture consists of a shared practices and understanding within a society. Since, the period of civilization the material culture of each people includes production designated through art. The artistic expression is done in an enormous varieties and forms. Gradually, with the implication of lyrics the arranged sentences tuned into the forms of songs. Simultaneously, with the song the mental expression created a correlationship with the physical appearances and attitudes which ultimately turned into dance. Both dance and songs are the expression of human thought where language is the media and way of approach to each other.

Dance locally known as '*jagoi*' is the most exquisite feature of the Manipuri culture. Its most important feature is the close association of religion with music and dance.

Manipuri dance is the collective name given to the dance and performance traditions that is the heritage of the Meitei people in Manipur. It has different elements in it. The classical tradition is the ones associated with Rasleela, and Natpala. The folk/indigenous elements are those from *Lai-haraoba*.

During the rule of King Pamheiba the development of classical Manipuri dance started (from 18th Century). King Jai Sing, an artist and a devotee of Lord Krishna succeeded in giving a new dimension to *Rasa Nritya* by blending traits from the folk dances and music of the surrounding territories of Manipur, i.e. Assam, Bengal. King Chandrakirti is another ruler and patron who helped development and promotion of Manipuri dance traditions brought about meaningful modification in the *Lai Haraoba* dance.

The cult of *Radha* and *Krishna*, particularly the *raslila*, is central to its themes but the dances, unusually, incorporate the characteristic symbols (*kartal* or *manjira*) and double-headed drum (*pung* or Manipuri *mridang*) of *sankirtan* into the visual performance.

Manipuri dance is purely religious and its aim is a spiritual experience. Development of music and dance has through religious festivals and daily activities of the Manipuri people. It is also a medium of worship and enjoyment, a door to the divine, but indispensable for all socio-cultural ceremonies. From the religious as well as from the artistic angle of vision, Manipuri

Fig. 3.1: Manipuri Dance form

Classical form of dance is claimed to be one on the most, modest and mildest and one of the most meaningful dances of the world.

Manipuri dance style is multifaceted and ranges from the softest feminine to the vigorous masculine. Dignified grace is found in every aspect and the range it offers in technique, rhythmic and tempo, which makes a Manipuri recital an absorbing and exhilarating experience. The movements of the body, feet and facial expressions in the dance are delicate and aspire to exhibit complete devotion and gracefulness.

The costumes for Manipuri dance are very attractive and the participants are attired in specified dresses.

The history of Manipuri dances may be classified into two broad categories: (a) Pre-Hindu (Pre-Vaishanvite); (b) Hindu (Vaishnavite). The two types are associated with religious motifs and mutually involve each other as we find them today.

The Important Manipuri Dance

Raslila

After Vaishnavism came into the valley of Manipur, the Manipuris accepted many of the themes and festivals that are celebrated throughout India but in Manipur there was a special element added to it, dance and music. At this juncture the repertoire of classical Manipuri dance came into existence, Raslila and Natpala began at this time.

The premiere Hindu dance tradition of Manipur is contained in the Manipuri Raslilas, which are night-long or day-long dance dramas about the life of Krishna that are held in the temple courtyards. The beautiful Raslila of the Manipuris were produced under the Patronage of Rajashree Bhagyachandra (1768-1798). The first Raslila dance was dedicated to Shree Shree Govindaji. There are four main types of Ras *viz*., Maharas, performed on the fullmoon day of *Hiyangei* (November), Kunjaras perform on the fullmoon of *Mera* (October), Vasantaras performed on the night of fullmoon of *Hiyangei* (November) and Nityaras with no specific time). The Raslila dance is centre around Lord Krishna's play with Radha and Gopis.

Emphasis on a particular episode songs, Ragas, Raginis are found differs from one category to another, e.g. Abir-Khel (play with sprinkling of coloured water) and appearance of Chandravali as Radha's rival is found only in Vasantaras. It is believed that the foundation of Ras, techniques, the costumes and ornaments, make-up etc. was revealed to Rajashree Bhagya Chandra in his dream.

Fig. 3.2: Raslila Dance with Lord Krishna in centre with Radha and Gopis

Krishna and Radha and her Consorts

This graceful and slow movement of the dance makes it one of the most acclaimed classical dances of India. The costume is elegant, as there are nicely embroidered clothes that give luster to the beauty of the art. The costumes for Krishna consist of a blue shirt with crown of flowers topped with fan like piece embossed with peacock feather, a silver colour flute with rings, bangles, bracelets, armbands for the hand and ornaments for the foot. The costumes and ornaments of Radha and Gopis consist of embroidered silk skirt, a blouse (*phurit*) of green colour for Radha and red colour for Gopis, a girdle round the waist and a veil thrown over the head with various ornaments on different parts of the body.

Pala Kirtana

Fig. 3.3: Pala Kirtana

Pala Kirtana singers in Turbans and Dhuties perform the *kirtan*. King Jaysingha is said to have initiated the present form of Pala Kirtan style.

Laiharaoba Jagoi

The *Laiharaoba* is a very ancient dance tradition of Meiteis. The Manipuri word for God is "Lai" for example "Lai Shang" means temple of God. "Laipaw" message of God etc. Similarly, "Lai Haraoba" means "Making merry with the Gods". It is performed generally after the harvest season. As stated in the sacred texts, the kings arranged this dance annually for imitating the play of Gods. It consists of several rituals and dance themes and the dance last for one to two weeks.

The premiere festival of the Pre-Hindu tradition on Manipur, the word *Lai-haraoba* has been derived from *lai hoi lauba* which literally means shouting of the word 'hoi' by the gods reflecting on the Meitei creation myth. There are four kinds of celebration of Lai-haraoba throughout Manipur: Kanglei haraoba (celebrated in the major parts of Manipur), Moirang haraoba (celebrated in Moirang), Chakpa haraoba (celebrated in Chakpa and the non-Hindu Meitei villages) and Kakching haraoba (celebrated in Kakching). Among these Kanglei haraoba is the most common form of celebration. The celebration of Lai-haraoba is done any time between April and June, and the celebration may last from one day to one month depending on the enthusiasm and monetary capacity of the organizers. It is usually celebrated communally collecting revenues from the community. The festival is dedicated to the local pre-Hindu deity of the area where it is celebrated, and is officiated by *maibas* (male priests), *maibis* (female priestesses) and the *pena-khongba* (the player of pena, a stringed instrument).

The mythological genesis of Lai-haraoba is very complex, and there are various stories around it. It is commonly believed that Lai-haraoba started in the Koubru hills (a sacred pilgrim, and all the gods of the Meitei pantheon participated in the festival. The mythologies are found in various hand-written manuscripts known as the *puyas*. The rituals of Lai-haraoba start with Lai-ikouba (waking up of the deity) from water on the first day. The daily proceedings include Lai-yakaiba (the awakening of the deities by singers with penas early morning), Laiman-phamba (when the maibis predicts the future). The evening rituals consist of Lei-langba (offering flowers to the deities by the common people), Hoi-laoba (singing by the maibis), Thougal-jagoi (dance with maibis to invoke the deities), Laiching jagoi (the maibis dance with the sequence involves a variety of expressive movements), Laibou-chongba (dance of creation) done by maibis, the sequence ends with Leiren mathek (a maiba indicates the movement of a snake in a single line which is a symbol of the snake-god Pakhangba); Wakol, (all the cultic objects are kept inside the temple) and then a concluding song is sung to put the deities to sleep. The Lai-haraoba ceremony also includes Lai-lamthokpa, in which the lais are put in a palanquin and taken out in a procession; Kanglei-thokpa (the maibi chooses the bride of the lai) and the all night function on the last night of Lai-haraoba, known as Lairoi. In this occasion the mythological story of Tangkhul and Nurabi are enacted by the Pena-khungba and the maibis. This story of this enactment is highly ritual in nature and symbolizes the propagation of fertility in the Meitei society. Lai-haraoba festival is identified to be the ideological roots of dance and theatre of Manipuri tradition. The dance of maibis and the ritual theatre of the lairoi numit is the oldest example of dance and traditional theatre among the Meiteis.

Fig. 3.4: Lai Haraoba dancers

The circular dance under the leadership of Maibis are participated by the village youth as well as married men and women is an important feature in Lai Haraoba dance. The songs which are sung during Lai Haraoba dance by the Maibis are very interesting one. At the end of Lai Haraoba, the Maibis pray to God for the welfare and prosperity of the community members of the locality.

Khamba and Thoibi Dance

In the mythology of Meiteis, the incarnation of the Thangjing God is known as "Moirang Saiyon". There are seven incarnations

Fig. 3.5: Khamba Thoibi dancers

of Thangjing god. Nongpok Ningthou and Panthoibi is the first and Khamba and Thoibi is the last incarnation.

Khamba Thoibi dance is a duet of male and female partners, a dance of dedication to the sylvan deity, Thangjing of Moirang. Khamba and Thoibi are actually two mythological characters who have become immortal in Manipuri folklore.

Pung Cholom (Mridanga)

Pung or Manipuri Mridanga or drum dance is the soul of Manipuri Sankritana music and Classical Manipuri Dance is a combination of sound and movement. It assumes an important ritual character, an indispensable part of all social and devotional ceremonies in Manipur, the instrument itself becoming an object of veneration. Pung Cholom is a highly refined classical dance number characterised by the modulation of sound from a soft whisper to a thunderous climax. There is the interplay of intricate rhythms and cross-rhythms with varying markings of time from the slow to the quick with graceful and vigorous body movements leading to ecstatic heights.

Fig. 3.6: Pung Cholom dancers

The Pung Cholom are performed either as an integral part of Nata San Kirtan with about 40 complicated Taals. The Pung Cholom players are all male and wears *dhoti*. They have a special type of turban which they chop by their flicking of head and movements.

Thabal Chongba

The word Thabal Chongba refers to dancing in moonlight. This is a very joyful dance performed by the youth as well as young married ones in the moonlight in an open field. The Manipuris have been performing this dance since pre-Vaishnavite period known as Keiyeb, (a dance Lord Pakhangba by joining hands of nine Gods and seven goddesses) and jumping anti clockwise so that Sanamahi (a tiger) cannot break the circle. In the Thabal-Chonga any member can participate and the dance is performed by holding hands between a male and a female. A trained singer and drum artist with Haribala (howl to god) sang religious song, historical ballads, epics of Moirang etc. and it continues for one to two weeks and the dancers dance to the tune of drums. In earlier times, Thabal-Chongba was performed with traditional dresses but now-a-days people dance with modern dresses like jeans and T-shirts. No special costumes for this dance. Thabal-Chongba dance is performed during February–April i.e., during *Basant Panchami*, Holi festival and Meitei New year. Another important feature of the Thabal-Chongba festival is that guys and girls get chance to interact with their love ones.

Fig. 3.7: Thabal Chongbi Dhance

Observation

For Manipuris dance is not just a form of art, but a way of life. Intensely devotional in mood, the Manipuri dances are a part of the daily life of the Manipuri people. Essentially presented as a group dance with gorgeous, colourful costumes and gentle, swaying petal-soft movements. Besides Rasalilas, there are other dances called Natasankirtana, in which a group of men play cymbals and dance in a circle or in two rows singing praises of God. In Pung Cholom, the dancers play upon pung, the drum, and dance while playing the intricate time cycles, executing somersault and breathtaking acrobatic feats. In group dances like Lai Haraoba, the merry-making for the gods, the dancers perform various steps and weave patterns, involving various choreographic compositions. From the corpus of Manipuri dances, one sees on the contemporary stage solo, duet and group performances. Maximum efforts need to be made to preserve the essence and authenticity of Manipuri dance.

References

Anthony, B., (1986), *Imphal*, MacMillar, London.

Grierson, Dr. G.A. *Report on the Linguistic Survey of India*, Vol. III, Parts II & III.

Grimwood, E., (1892), *My Three Years in Manipur*, Oxford, London.

Hodson, T.C. (1975), *The Meiteis*, Neeraj Publication House, Delhi.

Hodson, T.C. (1982), *Tribes of Manipur*, Oxford, London.

M'Cullock, Major W. (1859), *Account of the Valley of Manipoore.*

Namejrakpam, B. (2008), *A History of Neitrabak*, Moulana Offset Press, Hojai, Assam.

Rahman, S.A., (2006), *The Beautiful India Manipur*, Reference Press, New Delhi.

Selections from the Records of the Government of India, No. XXVIII, Calcutta.

4
History, Society and Culture of Medieval Assam in *Fat-he Ibriya*[1] of Shahabuddin Talish

T.H. Ansari

Fat-he Ibriya or Tarikh-I Assam gives quite interesting description about Assam and Cooch Behar during second half of the seventeenth century. It has one interesting chapter which deals with the geography, flora and fauna, natural resources, economic condition, the origin of the Assamese Muslims, arts and crafts, dress and customs of the people and some other aspects. Some of the descriptions given in this historical book may differ from the established fact but the most important thing is that we come through the notion that how this North East region has been perceived by the people who came to conquer it.

It appears that Talish had been completely unaware of the physical, social, cultural and political conditions of the lands he was visiting. The greenery and the physical resources attracted him, socio-cultural diversities amazed him and the climate conditions kept him awe-struck. In his description he is critical about some aspects of Assam but at the same time he appreciates other features of society. It may be noted that all medieval chronicles written by court scribes and other writers under the sponsorship of kings and generals throughout the world, are characterized by such subjectivity, with excessive praise of the sponsoring kings and generals and harsh and unsavory remarks against the opposite party.

According to *Fat-he Ibriya*, Assam is a dangerous and horrible land inhabited by the people on both sides of the Brahmaputra River.[2] The river flows from east to west and its east-west length from Guwahati to Sadna (Sadia) is 200 Karroh Jarib (one Karoh is equal to 1/3 of a Farsang and one Farsang is equal to 6 km.). Its north-southwise breadth from the mountain where the different tribal communities like Miri, Majami (Mishmis), Dafla and Landa (Naga) live to the Naga Hills is about a distance 7 to 8 days of hill journey.[3] The southern range of hills of this country consists of the Khasi, Chachar and Kashmir (perhaps Karbi) hills and adjoins the Naga hill in the east. The land lying to the northern side of the Brahamaputras is known as Uttarkul and on the southern side it is known as Dhakinkul. The area of Dhakinkul is stretched from Guwahati to the home of Miri community. The Dhakinkul starts from the area of Nakirani and ends at the village of Sadna.[4] The Miri and Majmi (Mishmi) tribes inhabit the hills situated in the eastern Assam of Uttarkul. This hill is at a distance of eleven days journey from the capital city of Kahargaon and is famous for musk deer, elephant, silver, lead and copper. The manner and custom of these tribes have similarity with those of the Assamese (Ahoms). But the women of these tribes are more beautiful and attractive than the Assamese women. They fear the gun very much. They believe that gun is a very bad thing. It makes noise without moving from its place. A child coming out from the stomach of the gun kills the human being.[5] The Nagas are a tribal community, who live in the southern hill ranges of Assam. They have fair and radish complexion. Outwardly, they are very good but very different inwardly. Judging by number they have even surpassed the group of Yujuj and Majuj (Gog and Magog, who according to Islam will appear on this earth before the advent of *Qeyamat*). They have bulky figure and strong physical structure. They, in hardiness and physical strength, are like the Aad Tribe (one of the Tribal communities of Arab).[6]

The land of Assam lies in the lap of eastern China. It is a different world, where its people and its geographical conditions are of different nature. The land is not like the other land and sky is not like the other sky. The sky is always full of clouds, which sometimes gives untimely rain. In this land, the humus becomes green without any external help. The land is very vast and its space is very expansive. The land of Assam is totally cut off from the main land. It doesn't have any fixed season. Sometimes it is winter during summer and sometimes summer during winter. Its roads are like the caves of death, and are full of danger and horror. Its bushes are full of thorn and injurious and harmful. Its rivers are similar to a thinking person, are very deep. Here Talish is not able to identify the region on the northern side of Assam and pointed out that Assam lies in the lap of eastern China. Although, the regions in the northern side of Assam are Bhutan and Arunachal Pradesh.

The people of Assam are like the pupils of a blind man's eyes that do not have any real sight. They are shy of a trip to other countries. They are like the poisonous plant in quality and use. The people of warfare are sharp shooters, great warriors and equally quarrelsome.[7] Anyone who came to this country never returned unless death overtakes him. An outsider does not know much about Assam and its people. The people of Hindustan describe the inhabitants of this land as magicians and consider them as beings out of pale of human race. They believe that this land is a land of magic and talisman. They say that whosoever goes to that country is charmed by magic, which prevents him from returning home.[8]

The entire population of this land does not follow any particular religion. Whatever eatable things they get from anybody they consume these without any consideration of caste, creed and religion. They performed every kind of work, which is good according to their individual opinion. They eat food prepared by anyone, be he a Muslim or a non-Muslim. They eat every kind of flesh except human flesh. It does not make any difference to them whether the animal meat they are eating is *Halal* or not.

They are not used to taking oil in their dishes. If by chance their food gives smell of oil they refrain from consuming it. The language of the country is entirely different from the language of the people who live in the eastern countries.[9] The male members are very bold and courageous. They know how to overcome the difficult situation. All of them are good fighters and blood thirsty. They are brave and fearless both in killing and losing their own life. They are unparalleled in cruelty, treachery and inhumanity. They are notorious in trick, falsehood and unfaithfulness.[10] They shave their head, beard and mustache. If someone is found violating this norm, he is put to death charging him for the following the custom of Bengal.[11]

Assamese women are beautiful and charming and have attractive body, black complexion, long and black hair, attractive hands and legs. From a distance they look very beautiful and charming, but seen from close they lack grace and charm. The wives of the Raja and also the common people do not cover their faces before anybody, and they move in the market with uncovered head. There are only a few persons who have only two wives. Otherwise majority of Assamese men have four to five wives. They sell, purchase and even barter their wives among each other. The general public while going before Raja and *Bhukans* kneel down as a mark of respect. When *Bhukans* visit the Raja first they kneel down and sit down with folded knee and keep their head lowered looking to the ground.[12] The Raja and *Bhukan* travel in the *Singhasan* and the well off and the chiefs on the *Doli* (Dola). The *Doli* looks very funny and is made of wooden board. The *Singhasan* is made of plain wood. A wooden chair tied on the back of an elephant is called *Hauda.*[13] The people of Assam generally put coarse cloth on the head, a *Chadar* on the shoulder and tie *Lungi* at the waist. The persons wear a kind of half coat during the winter. This coat is like our *Yaqubkhali* one. But those who hold a high position in the society sleep on bed instead of *charpoy*. The people eat lots of *Tamul* (betel nut) along with raw *supari.*[14]

The Rajas of this land are proud by reasons of the numerical superiority of their followers and retinues and large possession of their properties, treasure and a big army. They love to be surrounded by brave soldiers and gigantic elephants. The present king is Raja Jayadhawaj Singha titled Sarki (Swargadeo). The Sarki (Swargi) is a Hindi word, which means sky (heaven). There is a corrupt and mystified belief in the regard that one of the forefathers of this Raja was the sovereign ruler of the angles. He descended from the sky by a golden ladder and got engaged in organizing important affairs of this land. As he found this land so beautiful and prosperous that he declined to return to his original abode.

Verse

You have put affairs of the world so orderly and beautifully that even the sky is lauding you.[15] Six to seven thousand Assamese guard the palace of the Raja round the clock. They are known as Jodang (Chaudang). They are very faithful, main executioners and devoted servants of the Raja.[16]

The majority of the hill people (tribal people) do not pay any tribute to the Raja of Assam but they acknowledged his superiority and carry out some of his orders. However, the Naga tribe does not submit to the Raja and made raids into his territory. From the village of Kaliabor to the city of Kahargaon fruit trees surround every place and house. On either side of the road there are shady bamboo trees raising their height to the sky. Besides the cane field, there are cultivated lands and gardens up to the foot of the hills. The route from Lakhogarh to Kahargaon is inhabited and covered with cultivated land. A high and wide road has been constructed up to Kahargaon for the use of the people. The agricultural fields and gardens are planted so systematically in the plains in this country that one cannot see any depression or elevation in the field. *Uttarkol* is more cultivated and more flourishing than *Dakhinkol*. But from administration and strategic advantage, *Dakhinkol* is more suitable for living. As the kings of

Assam have always been residing on this side. The climatic condition of the territories nearer the bank of Brahamaputra is equally suitable for both natives and foreigners. But the climate of the area away from the Brahamaputra River is comfortable and suitable only to the native people; otherwise it is like the venom of a snake for the strangers. Rain continues incessantly for eight months but it rains occasionally during the four months of winter.[17]

Assam has a variety of flowers and fruits which also grow in Hindustan and Bengal. However, other varieties of flowers and fruits, both wild and cultivated, noticed in this country are not found in any part of Hindustan. These wild and cultivated flowers bloom and add fragrance to the gardens. The coconut and *Neem* trees are somewhat rare. But the coconut is sweet, juicy and tasty. There are three kinds of sugarcane: black, red and yellow. All are very sweet but very hard to chew. Gingers are very big, soft, and fibreless and have good flavour. *Panyal*, a variety of *Amla,* is so delicious and tasty that men of taste prefer it to damson. The chief crop of Assam is paddy. But the thin and finer variety of rice is rare. Wheat, barley and lentil are not cultivated in this land. Though its soil is so fertile that whatever is cultivated or planted grows very fast and in abundance.[18]

Many kinds of birds like duck, goose and fighting cock are found in this country. Their meat is very delicious and tasty. It was observed that when a thin and weak cock is pitted against a big and strong cock, it fights courageously and boldly and does not turn away its face from enemy even though its head is broken or it is half dead. Among the animals, gigantic and dreadful elephant, deer, stag, *nilgaye*, ram and francolin are found both in mountains and in plains. One can also find he-goat and she-goat. In the capital city of Kahargaon some cage like small but very strong structures supported by heavy wooden posts at the four corners, are constructed. It appears that these are used for different purposes. On enquiry it was found that there was some expert *Mahawats* (elephant keepers) of the Raja who rubbed a particular herb on the body of a female elephant. Then she was carried to graze in the grazing grounds, where wild and tusk elephants live. As soon as the tusk elephant smelt that herb rubbed on the female elephant, it became mad and followed her. Then the *Mahawat* skilfully brings back the female elephant to the cage like structure. The moment the tusk elephant enters the enclosure it is trapped to be trained and domesticated later on.[19] Donkies, camels and horse are very rare in Assam. The people of this country, who are ignorant of these strange animals, love to have and see these animals again and again. They, due to their stupidity, purchase donkey at very high prices. They become very delighted and overjoyed after seeing one of the rare creations of God that is a camel. They are very much afraid of horses. If they, by chance, find this animal, chop its leg immediately. If one horseman attacks one hundred Assamese they take flight by throwing away their arms. Those who could not run away surrender before the rider. But, if one Assamese catches ten Muslim foot soldiers, he invariably becomes desperate, unless he overcomes them. The people of Assam consider selling of elephant as extremely shameful and disgraceful act and do not approve this.[20] The people are very expert weavers and knit beautiful clothes of silk and velvet. They are also expert carpenters and make very decent and comfortable furniture such as box, cot, *diwan* and chair from a single piece of timber without sawing the wood. Some of the cots made by expert carpenters from one block of wood are found in the palace of Raja. It was two *Zerya* wide (one *zerya* is equal to 104 centimetre). The leg was also made of the same block of wood without cutting it separately.[21] The houses of Assam were not constructed with brick, stone and mud except some gates at Kahargaon and some places of worship. Generally, the poor and rich people construct their houses with wood, reed and grass.[22]

The people of Assam used the weapons like the gun, the matchlocks, and the cannon, the pointed and rough arrows with iron heads, *daos,* long spears and bow made of bamboo. At the time of war, entire population of the land including professionals, indigenous people, new settlers, Hindus and Muslims, all willingly or unwillingly take very active part in the battle. They attack the enemy united like the jackals and the hyenas. They behave like foxes that terrorize the tigers of the forest and crocodiles of the deep water from their clamour and noise and compel them to leave the battlefield. Majority of the Assamese would like to be always in the forefront in the battlefield. But those courageous soldiers who fight bravely and valiantly with the enemy with their sword and arrow are mainly indigenous people. They consist of twenty thousand young men only. Most of the times they prefer to go for battle and raid on the night of Tuesday. They consider night as very auspicious. Those who get defeated while fighting or without fighting, always remember this proverb, "life is precious than death" and retreat hastily after throwing down the arms which they had brought for battle.[23] The people bury their dead with some of their patrimonial properties keeping the head towards the east and leg towards the west. The noble and high-ranking officers prepare funeral vaults (*maidams)* for their dead and also put some utensils made of gold and silver, carpet, dress materials and eatable items necessary for a period of several years inside it. They also put wives and servants of a dead person inside the same burial chamber after having killed them. They fixed the head of the dead person tightly with a strong wooden pole. One lamp with plenty of oil and a torchbearer is placed alive into the vault (*maidams*). The job of the torchbearer is to look after the lamp so that it cannot get extinguished. Later on when ten such crypts were excavated valuable items worth nine thousand rupees were found in them. It was very surprising to discover one golden pendant from the grave of a queen as old as eighty years. Surprisingly the *pan* leaves (betel) of that pendant were still green. Though the writer did not see the *pan* leaves himself, he had heard about it from Payande Beg, an appointed *Waqeya Newis*, and Shah Beg, who officially supervised the excavation process, in the presence of *Nawab*, who is above all the titles. The *Darogha* of treasury, Rasmi Big to whom the pendant was handed over to testify it, he told that the pendant was pure.[24]

Talish is giving some details about the origin of the Assamese Muslims. Once Hussain Shah, one of the sultans of Bengal invaded Assam with twenty thousand cavalry and foot soldiers. The Raja of Assam left his country and fled to the mountains. Hussain Shah having left his own son with a large army to control this country returned to Bengal. As soon as the rainy season arrived and all the routes were blocked, the Raja came down from the mountain and slew the Prince, the son of Hussain Shah. The army of the Prince proved to be ineffective in a very short time. All of them either killed or taken prisoner. It is said that one group among the inhabitants of this country having Muslims names, are descendants of those prisoners of war.[25] They married local women according to their choice. Their children now have accepted the manners and customs of the Assamese people. They are Muslims in name only and had nothing to do with Islam. They are more inclined to be associated with the local people than the Muslims. But one group of Muslims who had settled down earlier thereby leaving the land of Islam performs *Namaz,* observe *Roza* with full devotion and religious zeal. But they were not allowed to call *Aazan* and read the *Quran* aloud.[26]

The entire city of Garhagaon, is fortified with cane fields. The width of the cane field was around two to three *karoh*. The capital complex is built without any proper planning. The residential houses are constructed haphazardly giving a very ugly look. Some people even have constructed their houses in the cane field near the road. Everyone has a garden and cultivated land in front of his house. The cultivated lands are between the road and the house. A river named *Dikhow* flows by the king's palace. The banks of this river are thickly inhabited. There is also a market near the bank of the river where only the *Pan* sellers sit.[27] The inhabitants of this land do not buy any foodstuff from the shop. They cultivate and store everything in their houses sufficient for one year. They do not like to buy and sell any eatable items too. This capital city, Kahargaon occupies a very large area. It seems that this habitation consists of so many villages. There is a wide road around the king's palace. The bamboo fences and a ditch surround this road. The ditch is deeper than the height of a man and is always full of water. The compound of king's palace is spread over one *Karoh* and fourteen *Jarib* of land.[28]

The writer has given very interesting description of one audience hall of the king's palace locally known as Soolang which is 120 cubits in length and 30 cubits in breadth. It is supported by 66 wooden posts which is four *Zera* (around 104 centimetre) in thickness. The posts were polished in such a manner as it appears that it has been carved out with the help of machine. Though the people of Assam claimed that these posts prepared with the help of machine but the reason and logic do not fit into support it. The other crafts and novelties used by the carpenters in decorating these wooden posts of the king's palace are beyond my description. There is no one in this universe that can construct, design or decorate wooden houses like the people of Assam. Besides the king's palace there were other beautiful, comfortable and clean houses for the stay of the Raja. The Bukhans also lived in stylish and well built houses near the Raja's palace. Those Bhukans, who had matrimonial relation with the Raja, live in beautiful houses surrounded by fresh and well laid out gardens and ponds full of clean and sweet water. It was really an enhancing and an attractive palace. Due to the heavy humidity, the people of this land do not sit or sleep on the ground; but they prepare *Machan* (raising platform of wood) and live on it only.[29]

We also find a good description of diseases in *Tarikh- I Assam*. During cold season, various diseases caused by the humid weather are more hostile to the foreigners than the natives. During the summer, deadly diseases like jaundice make outsiders their victims more than the native people. But the people of this land generally do not suffer from different fatal diseases like leprosy, white leprosy, elephantiasis, varicose veins, pharyngitis, and other contagious diseases of skin that are very common in Bengal. Otherwise also, the people of this land are free from other chronic diseases. The air and water of the hills are equally deadly and poisonous to the natives and strangers as well. This land is surrounded by the hills so the weather is very uncomfortable.

The trees of its hills and dry lands are very high, thick and strong. There are numerous rivers with and without swamp.[30]

Salt is very dear and difficult to obtain. The salt is found at the foot of certain hills; but it tests very bitter and also of caustic nature. Some natives of this country cut the young banana trees and dry them in the sun. Then they are burnt and the ashes are kept in a canvas bag. The canvas bag packed with the ashes is put on a high platform and water is poured over it. In this process it is distilled and used as salt though it is very acidic.[31] Here Talish has observed very minutely about the preparation of salt by the local people.

The gold is sifted out from the sand of Brahmaputra. Around ten to twelve thousand men are engaged in this work. Each of them has to deposit one *Tòla* of gold annually to the treasury of the Raja. But this gold is considered of substandard in quality. One *Tòla* of gold is sold for eight to nine rupees only. It is said that the gold is found everywhere in the sand of Brahamaputra. But only the people of Assam know the exact location where gold is found. The currency of Assam consists of cowries, silver rupees and *Ashrafi* (golden coin). The copper coins are not accepted here.[32]

No foreigners ever ruled this country in the past. A stranger never put his foot of domination on this land. The entrance and the exit points are very narrow for the outsiders. Likewise the inhabitants of this land are shy of a trip to other countries. The Raja neither allows foreigners to enter Assam nor does he permit his own subjects to go out of his kingdom. Before the conflict that took place between Assamese and the Mughals, the Assamese used to come near the border of Guwahati once in a year, with the permission of their Raja to carry out business. They brought products like gold, musk, aloe-wood, pepper, *Sazaj* and silk clothes and bartered them for salt, sulphur, brimstone and some other Indian goods imported by the traders of Guwahati. In short any invader who entered the boundary of this kingdom could hardly go back alive. Any caravan that set foot on this land took abode in the world of no return. Earlier whenever invaders set out to occupy Assam they faced frequent night raids carried out by the local inhabitants on the border. If their night raids did not yield the desired result, then they moved in to the hills along with the entire population. They did not leave any sign of habitation in that area. The opponent totally unaware of this dreadful strategy, on reaching the heart of the country after crossing the treacherous and terrible rivers, dangerous forests full of bloodthirsty thorns, faced cold freezing weather besides incessant rain and annihilation. Once the rainwater started rolling down from the top of the hills the inhabitants would come down from the hill to surround the enemy. It is said that for a damp mud a single drop of water is enough to bring disaster. As a result the careless opponents surrounded on all sides by the locals, finally lose morale to fight or to defend themselves. They feel helpless and become disabled and in a very short time either got killed or taken prisoner. In this manner, a large, powerful and dignified armed force, caught in a horrible whirlpool was decimated in the depth of river.[33]

Verse

In this desert every thorn is like a finger, which guides the people.
And every chirping of a nightingale is familiar.[34]

Notes

1. *Fat-he Ibriya or Tarikh-I Assam* written by Shahabuddin Talish describes the social and political history of the period of Swargadeo Jaidhwaj Singha, especially of the period from 1661 to 1663. Talish accompanied Mir Jumla's invading army, who made incursion deep into Ahom kingdom and captured Garhgaon, the capital, and kept it under their subjugation for about one year. Although the book gives generally the accounts of attacks, sieges, chases and fighting on land and water between Mir Jumla's forces and Ahom forces, but it also describes the then socio-economic, political and cultural environment of Assam. (I have consulted Tarikh-I Assam both in

Persian as well as English tr. By Mazhar Asif, published by Department of Historical and Antiquarian Studies, Guwahati, 2009).

2. Shahabuddin Talesh, *Fat-he Ibriya*, (Persian), Calcutta, 1849, p. 56.
3. *Fat-he Ibriya,* p. 56.
4. *Fat-he Ibriya,* p. 56.
5. *Ibid*., pp. 62-63.
6. *Ibid*., p. 77.
7. *Ibid*., pp. 56-57.
8. *Ibid*., pp. 57-58.
9. *Fat-he Ibriya*, p. 68.
10. *Ibid*., pp. 68-69.
11. *Ibid*., p. 69.
12. *Ibid*.
13. *Ibid*., p. 70.
14. *Ibid*., pp.70-71.
15. *Fat-he Ibriya,* pp. 67-68.
16. *Ibid*., pp. 72-73.
17. *Ibid*., p. 59.
18. *Ibid*., p. 62.
19. *Fat-he Ibriya*, p. 63.
20. *Ibid*., pp. 69-70.
21. *Ibid*., pp. 71-72.
22. *Ibid*., p. 73-74.
23. *Fat-he Ibriya*, pp. 74-75.
24. *Ibid*. pp. 75-76.
25. *Ibid*., pp. 65-66.
26. *Fat-he Ibriya,* pp. 76-77.
27. *Ibid*., pp. 77-78.
28. *Ibid*., p. 78.
29. *Ibid*., pp.78-79.
30. *Fat-he Ibriya,* pp. 59-60.
31. *Ibid*., pp. 60-61.
32. *Ibid*., pp. 62-63.
33. *Fat-he Ibriya*, pp. 65-66.
34. *Ibid*., pp. 65-66.

SECTION 2 : HEALTH STATUS OF NORTH EAST INDIA

5

Indigenous Healthcare Practices among the Karbis of Assam

A Study on the Role of Women

Reena Terangpi, Ni-et Teronpi, Hemphi Terangpi and *Robindra Teron*

Introduction

Indigenous or Traditional healthcare practice is an expression of traditional knowledge which has been developed through long years of association with nature and meticulous analysis of environmental features. Traditional knowledge is a "cumulative body of knowledge and beliefs handed down through generations by cultural transmission, about the relationship between man and his environment" (Berkes, 1993). These sophisticated set of understandings, interpretations and meanings are part and parcel of cultural complex that encompasses language, naming and classification systems, resource use practices, ritual, spirituality and worldview (Science and Traditional knowledge; ICSU, 2002). Indigenous healthcare systems, therefore, are not only useful for the conservation of the cultural traditions and biodiversity but also for primary community healthcare and drug development. In many developing countries traditional medicines occupy the first line of defence in primary healthcare. Traditional medicines have been extensively studied for anticancer property while in many African countries AIDS/HIV patients live on traditional medicines. World Health Organisation (WHO) define traditional medicine as a sum total of knowledge skill and practices based on theories, beliefs and experiences of different indigenous cultures, whether explicable or not, used in the maintenance of health and in the prevention, diagnosis, improvement and treatment of physical and mental illness or maintain well-being. According to WHO, more than 80 per cent of the world's population relies on traditional medicine for their primary healthcare needs (Traditional Medicine Strategy, 2002-2005).

Indigenous healthcare systems also referred as Traditional Medicine (TM) is prevalent among the Karbis, a prominent ethnic group in Assam, as first line of primary healthcare. The healthcare practice is based on their religious worldview and includes both medicines and rituals to cure scores of ailments. Ritual being an integral part of religion, therefore, its practice contributes towards expression of their culture. There are various factors, among them poverty, lack of medical facilities and ignorance are the main drivers of continuation of traditional medicine or local healthcare practice. From religious standpoint, healthcare is a continuous process which is observed during good times also. For example, being kind and doing no harm to others is a kind of noble deeds said to be appreciated by deities. Regular propitiations of deities and ancestor worship are said to please them and in return does no harm to the family. Faulty funeral rites is said to cause harm by gods, therefore, proper funeral rites prevents the family from causing harm by gods. There are many such examples. In case when the cause of illness is not known, a wise man or priest is consulted who by the act of divination (*sang kelang*) identify the cause of the disease. The role of women in primary healthcare is vital and at times eclipses that of men. Their involvement is not limited to healthcare but in various spheres of intangible cultural heritage such as language, codes of ethics, behavioural patterns, value systems and religious beliefs. Women are also custodians of intangible cultural heritage which encompasses, among other forms, the performing arts including music, culinary and medicinal knowledge and the know-how for the creation of material culture.

Karbis represents one of the prominent tribes of Karbi Anglong district (25°30′ to 26°36′ N and 92°90′ to 93°54′ E) in Assam state. The district comprises two detached parts (Fig. 5.1), the western part also referred as the Hamren sub-division with its headquarter at Hamren and the eastern part comprising Diphu and Bokajan sub-division with their respective headquarters at Diphu and Bokajan. Ethnically, Karbis are Mongoloid and linguistically belong to the Tibeto-Burman and more particularly the Kuki-Chin sub-group languages. Karbis have settlements in all the sister states of North East India as well as in Bangladesh, particularly the Chittagong Hill tracts. Due to lack of written history, not much is known about the origin of the Karbis. They are believed to have migrated from the Kuki-Chin area in and around the Chindwin river valley in western Myanmar (Lyall, 1908; Dutt, 1979; Bhattacharjee, 1986; Phangcho, 2001). Karbis

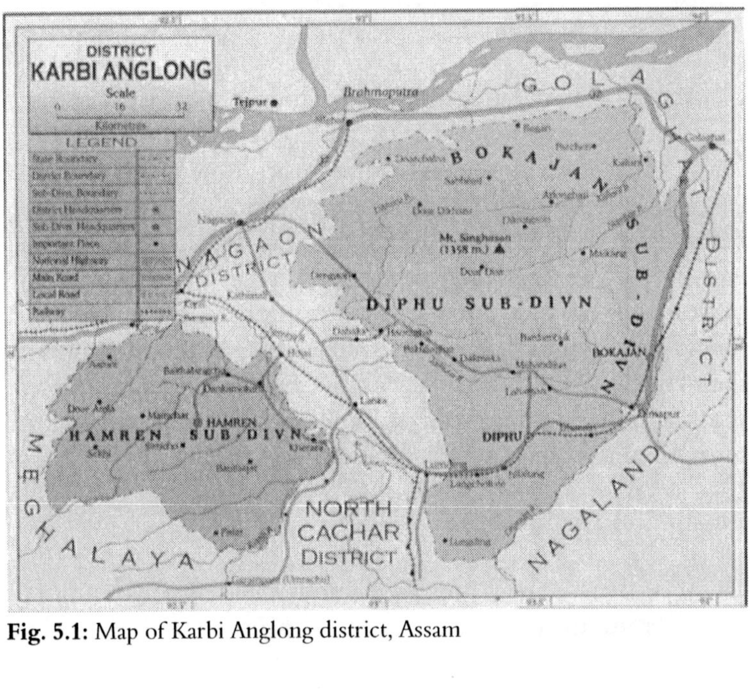

Fig. 5.1: Map of Karbi Anglong district, Assam

follow patrilineal system of family and belief in animistic form of religion in which rituals and ancestor worship form integral part. Further, they believe in immortality of souls and rebirth. Karbis are agriculturists and slash and burn is still the main mode of agriculture, at least in the hills.

Ethnobotanical study among the Karbis is a recent development. Actual botanical work in Karbi Anglong district was undertaken by Borthakur and Jain in 1970s and several research papers have been published by them (Borthakur, 1976a, 1976b, 1981a, 1981b, 1997a & b; Jain and Borthakur, 1980). Teron (2005, 2006), Teron and Gogoi (2004) and Gogoi *et al.* (2005) had reported a few accounts pertaining to the ethnobotany and traditional knowledge of the Karbis. These reports, however, are not exhaustive as health practices of the Karbis, which have been in existence since the days of yore, have not been discussed. In light of these, an attempt has been made by the present authors to document healthcare practices and their herbal prescriptions.

Materials and Methods

Field study was undertaken during September 2011 to February 2013 on indigenous healthcare practices among the Karbis in Karbi Anglong district. Information was collected from elders of 25 randomly selected villages. Informants included both men and women of different ages and unstructured interview method was used. We attended rituals, social occasions, etc. to make personal observations of information provided by informants. Traditional healers and priests were also consulted for sharing their knowledge on primary healthcare and their relationship with religion. Village elders and key informants were apprised of the purpose of the study and their consent is taken.

Result and Discussions

Traditional medicine is prevalent among the Karbis, a prominent ethnic group in Assam, as first line of primary healthcare. The healthcare practice is based on their religious worldview which considers diseases are the manifestation of God's displeasure over human violation of the divine will and propitiation is said to appease these gods and cure the patient. Indigenous medication to cure scores of ailments includes *kapherem* (charms), *kecho* (oral therapy), *kachekok, alek* (aroma therapy), *kachihi* (local application), *seh karkli* (rituals) and *kangduk* (ancestor worship). Karbis also use medicinal plants alone or in combination with occult practices. The present paper reported use of 30 (thirty) plants or its products (Table 5.1), 4 (four) animals or its parts and 4(four) minerals (Table 5.2) in indigenous healthcare system. Treatment of 4 (four) disease conditions using minerals were also discussed. Traditional medicines appear to be more intense in places where access to modern medical facilities is not in places and among poor section of the community. Birth attendants continue to play a major role in healthcare among rural folk. Traditional medicine though may not satisfy modern principles of science, it is an invaluable local knowledge system developed as a result of human interactions with nature, their beliefs, myths and religious practices.

Indigenous Healthcare Practices among the Karbis

Traditional worldviews and Concept of disease: Karbis believe in multiple gods (*Arnam*) and regard all objects (trees, stones, rivers, mountains, hills, etc.) on earth as incarnation of some deities and therefore, possess divinity. They believe diseases as the manifestation of God's displeasure over human violation of the divine will and propitiation of these gods is said to appease them and cure the patient. Two categories of gods or deities are recognised—*Arnam* (God) is good while *Hi-i* (evil) is usually bad, but considers both entities as possessing divinity and unseen power and enjoying equal status. In many Karbi families, however, evils are propitiated as *hem angtar* (Household God). For instance the God *Peng* (the Protector) which is actually a *Chekkama,* an evil figure, is propitiated by sacrificing black male goat and fowls.

Table 5.1: Plants used in indigenous healthcare system of the Karbi community

Sl. No	Botanical Name	Local Name	Part Used	Method of Treatment	Diseases
1.	*Acorus calamus* L. (Araceae)	*Chopi-u, Lang abab*	Roots	Aroma therapy	Stomach ailment and body pain.
2.	*Allium sativum* L. (Liliaceae)	*Harsun-kelok*	Scaly Leaves	Local application	Fever and cough.
3.	*Areca catechu* L. (Arecaceae)	*Kove*	Fruits	Local application	To heal the wound caused by detachment of placenta.
4.	*Arum* Sp. L. (Araceae)	*Hen*	Petiole	Local application	To heal cuts or injuries.
5.	*Aristolochia indica* Roxb. (Aristolochiaceae)	*Re-etso*	Leaves	Local application	*Ahop* characterized by symptom of loose motion with greenish excreta.
6.	*Brassica campestris* L. (Brassicaceae)	*Jangmu*	Seeds	Local application	Ward off evil spirit or nightmare.
7.	*Cajanus cajan* L. (Papilionaceae)	*Thekek*	Tender leaves	Oral application	For treatment of dysentery
8.	*Carica papaya* (Caricaceae)	*Mensopi*	Roots	Aroma therapy	For treatment of jaundice.
9.	*Citrus sp.* L. (Rutaceae)	*Tungmeng*	Leaf	Local application	Stomach Disorder
10.	*Curcuma longa* L. (Zingiberaceae)	*Tharmit*	Rhizome	Local application	Healing of wounds.
11.	*Cynodon dactylon* Pers. (Poaceae)	*Bap duburibon*	Leaves	Local application	For treatment of jaundice.
12.	*Dendrocalamus hamiltonii* Nees. (Poaceae)	*Jintak*	Bamboo Split	Local application	Use for cutting placental tube after child delivery
13.	*Eryngium foetidum* L. (Apiaceae)	*Vorek-jokasu*	Leaves	Oral application	Treatment of common cold
14.	*Gossipium herbaceum* Linn. (Malvaceae)	*Phelo*	Fibres	Local application	To drive away evil spirit.

(Contd.)

Table 5.1: *(Contd.)*

Sl. No	*Botanical Name*	*Local Name*	*Part Used*	*Method of Treatment*	*Diseases*
15.	*Jatropha curcas* L. (Euphorbiaceae)	*Bonbera*	Twig	Local application	Treatment of ringworm
16.	*Mimosa pudica* Linn. (Mimosaceae)	*Bap therak*	Roots	Oral with charm	Rabies
17.	*Mirabilis jalapa* L. (Nyctaginaceae)	*Hunmili-amir*	Roots	Local application	Snake bite
18.	*Musa paradisiaca* L. (Musaceae)	*Nusador*	Roots	Aroma therapy	For treatment of jaundice.
19.	*Ocimum killimandscharicum* Gurke. (Lamiaceae)	*Lopong*	Leaves	Local application	Parasite of fowls sticking in the naval.
20.	*Oryza sativa* L. (Poaceae)	*Sank*	Grains	Oral application	For treatment of diarrhoea
21.	*Papaver somniferum* L.; (Papaveraceae)	*kani*	Buds	Oral application	For treatment of Dysentery
22.	*Phaseolus aureus* Roxb. (Leguminasae)	*Chuphe*	Seed rind	Oral application with charm	To combat against filarial worm.
23.	*Phyllanthus acidus* Skeels (Euphorbiaceae)	*Takari thelu*	Bark	Oral application	For treatment of Dysentery
24.	*Piper betle* L. (Piperaceae)	*Bithi*	Leaves	Local application	Treatment of infection on naval
25.	*Piper* sp. L (Piperaceae)	*Bikron okso*	Leaves	Local application with charm	Treatment of excessive dripping of saliva.
26.	*Piper nigrum* L. (Piperaceae)	Black pepper	Fruits	Oral application.	Treatment of common cold.
27.	*Psidium gaujava* L. (Myrtaceae)	*Soprim*	Tender leaves	Oral application	Treatment of dysentery
28.	*Serrata chirayita* Roxb. Ex. Flam (Gentianaceae)	*Serrata*	Tender shoots	Oral application	Treatment of dysentery
29.	*Wrightia arborea* Dennst. (Apocynaceae)	*Bengvoi*	Bark	Oral application	Treatment of dysentery
30.	*Zingiber officinale* Rosc. (Zingiberaceae)	*Hanso*	Rhizome	Oral with charms	Sticking Back Pain/sleeplessness

Table 5.2: Minerals and Animals/Animal products used in indigenous healthcare system among the Karbis

Sl. No.	*Materials/Minerals/ Scientific names*	*Local name*	*Parts used/Product*	*Method of treatment*	*Diseases*
1.	*Apis mellifera* L. (Apidae)	Honey bee	Honey	Oral application	Mouth ulcer
2.	Charcoal	*Hokvai*	Charcoal	Local application	Navel pain
3.	Calcium hydroxide	Lime	Lime	Local application	To heal the wound caused by detachment of the placenta
4.	*Gallus gallus domesticus* L. (Phasianidae)	Rooster	Blood, liver, feathers and intestine	Propitiation	Appeasement of household and non-house hold Gods
5.	Rice beer *Oryza sativa* L. (Poaceae)	*Hor-lank*	95% alcohol	Oral application	Stomach ailment
6.	*Manis crassicaudata* Grey. (Manidae)	Pangolin/*Karpu*	Scales	Aroma therapy	Excessive saliva dripping
7.	*Philosomia ricini* Hutt. (Saturnidae)	Eri silk worm	Cocoon	Local application	To drive evil spirit
8.	Sickle	*Nokek rangso*	Curved blade	Oral charm	Ringworm in toes

Karbis have their own way of looking at illness and treating the patient. When a person falls ill after coming from forest, the family attributes the cause due to encounter of evil spirit(s). Prolonged illness without the influence of evils spirits is believed to be caused by household gods due to various reasons like irregular propitiations and violation of taboos related with the deity concerned. Every deity is said to manifest an illness with unique symptoms where conscious family elders can identify. In case the patient does not respond positively to commonly practised treatments, a wise man is consulted to determine the cause of the illness. The wise man through his divinity, identifies the deity responsible for the illness and suggest the family to perform certain rituals for recovery of the patient. This act of divinity by the wise man is called *Sang Kelang* (Fig. 5.2). Karbis also strongly believe in appeasement of their ancestors and honour them by offering feast. Such offering is done not only for good health but also for prosperity in life.

Fig. 5.2: A wise man performing *Sang Kelang* (divination); by such practice the practioner predict the cause of disease

Common Healthcare Practices

Rural Karbis still depend on traditional medicine and practices for primary healthcare. The healthcare system involves both uses of medicine, plants, animals and minerals and magico-religious practices; a few such commonly healthcare practises are briefly discussed below.

***Kapherem* (Charms):** In this category, the witch or wise man or wise women, would charm/incantations in order to cure a particular disease. The ailment is said to get cured only with the incantations because it is said to be associated with the deity. In such practice no medicine is prescribed by the medicine man. Examples include sore eyes, cuts, itchy toes and finger, allergic of caterpillar hair, burning sensations etc.

***Kachi-hi* (Local application)**: This category of practices may or may not involve use of charms by the practitioner. Practices involving charms are used for curing *Sor* (sticking back pain), headache, chronic secretion of saliva, to ward off evil spirit, etc. Local applications without charms are used against reptile bites, acidity, minor stomach ailment etc.

***Kecho* (Oral application)**: Supplement of oral medicines along with *kapherem* (charms) constitutes the Oral therapy. Common example includes treatment of rabies, cough, mouth ulcer, diarrhoea, jaundice, etc. by medicine such as antidote and pharyngeal problems are first subjected to charms and then given to patient.

***Kachekok* (Aroma therapy)**: This practice of child-care uses certain plants or plant parts in the form of an amulet or tied around the waist. Here, also the charms may or may not be used by the medicine man. Constipation, treatment of jaundice, excessive secretion of saliva, back-pain etc. are often healed through aroma therapy.

***Seh-karkli* (Rituals):** Long term illness if not cured by medicines, a diviner is consulted who with his divinity determines the deities to cure the patient. This act of divinity is called

Sangkelang and accordingly propitiation is done by sacrificing rooster or animals and is called *seh-karkli.* In case the patient suffers for long and do not respond to commonly practised treatment, a wise man is called or approached to identify the causes of the disease. The wise man by virtue of his divine act identifies the deity responsible for the disease and accordingly advice the family to do the needful. This act of divinity is called *Sang kelang* or rituals dedicated to the identified deity are called *Seh-karkli* which often involves sacrificing animals.

***Kangduk* (Ancestor worship)**: Karbis believe that the soul of the deceased member of the family remains in the house and influence functioning of the family. Deceased ancestors called *Teri-teram* are honoured by sacrificing fowls and pigs which is done for well-being and prosperity. This practice is called *kangduk*. Further, *teri-teram* are remembered and offered rice beer on important occasions like ritual of supreme deity or *Arnam kethe* and *Peng,* marriage and sometimes owning of new properties (cows, buffaloes, cars, etc.) in the family.

Common Ailments of Children and Their Treatment

For maintaining sound mental and physical health: The family elder calls the *kurusar* (priest) to perform *vur-matha* or a ritual dedicated to the deity *Hemphu*. It is usually performed when the child is found to be mentally depressed and absent-minded. This ritual is said to make the child mentally and physically strong and healthy and prevent influence of evil spirit.

Infection on navel: Sometimes, parasites of fowl invade the navel causing infection on it. To combat this ectoparasites leaves of *lopong* (*Ocimum kilimandscharicum* Gurke; family Lamiaceae) is crushed and paste is applied on the navel for quick recovery (Fig. 5.3). For *Bud* or navel pain, elders use to take *Hokwai* or charcoal from furnace and apply it on the navel which is claimed to reduce pain.

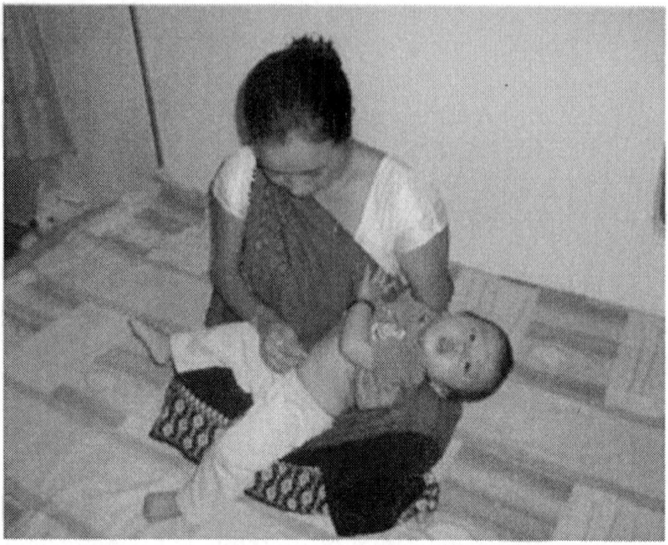

Fig. 5.3: A woman treating navel infection of child using leaves of *lopong* (*Ocimum kilimandscharicum*)

***Ahop* (symptoms of loose motions with greenish excreta)**: *Ahop* is the most common condition/ailment among infants. It is characterised by loose motions with greenish excreta. *Ahop*, however, is considered a regular phenomenon and the child show developmental changes after every occurrence of *ahop*. Leaves of *Re-etso* (*Aristolochia indica* Roxb.; family Aristolochiaceae) are crushed and applied on the head of new born baby during bath to prevent occurrence of such symptoms.

According to religious practice a wise man ties a bronze ring with cotton yarn, uses charm and the patient wears it around the neck. For boys, six number of thread are taken and damps it with a little amount of dew drops obtained from plants at dawn.

Birsi arkam: Children usually at the age of 1-7 suffer from excessive dripping of saliva from the mouth which results in reddish burning chin symptom locally called *Birsi arkam*. For this, wise man/woman uses oral charms and wipe the chin thoroughly with leaves of *Bikron okso* (*Piper* sp. L; family-Piperaceae). One leaf is used in a day and the treatment is continued for six days in case of boys and five days for girls. Besides, scale of pangolin or *Karpu* (*Manis crassicaudata* Grey; family Manidae) is worn as an amulet to cure this human condition (Fig. 5.4).

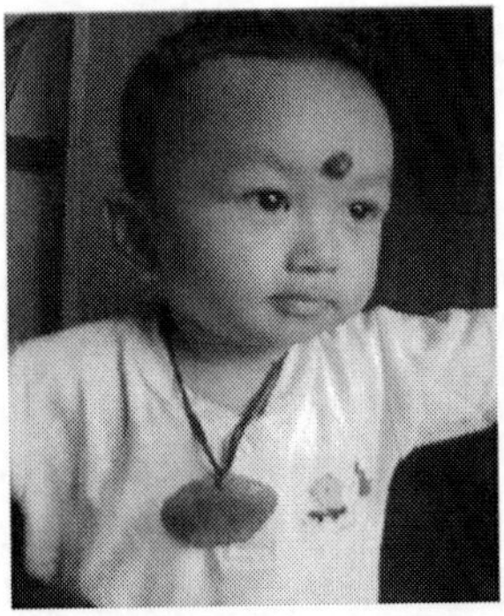

Fig. 5.4: Scales of pangolin worn as an amulet to cure *Birsi Arkam*

Sialorrhea: This symptom is characterised by excessive secretion of saliva and found to be common in children. A wise man is called upon to predict the cause of the ailment through *sang-kelang*. It is believed that a child suffers from *Sialorrhea* if the mother is deprived eatables of her choice during pregnancy. As per advice of the wise man, eatables of choice of the mother are provided to the child.

Common cold: Generally, traditional practice involves the use of mustard oil heated with garlic which is often rubbed all over the body and is said to heal the disease. Juice extracted from the paste of the leaves of the holy basil mixed with honey is frequently given to the patient suffering from such illness. This is said to cure the disease in a very rapid manner. A soup prepared with pieces of ginger and crushed black pepper (*Piper nigrum* L.; family Piperaceae) along with *vorek jokasu* or *Eryngium foetidum* L. (family Apiaceae) is given to patient suffering from such respiratory illness.

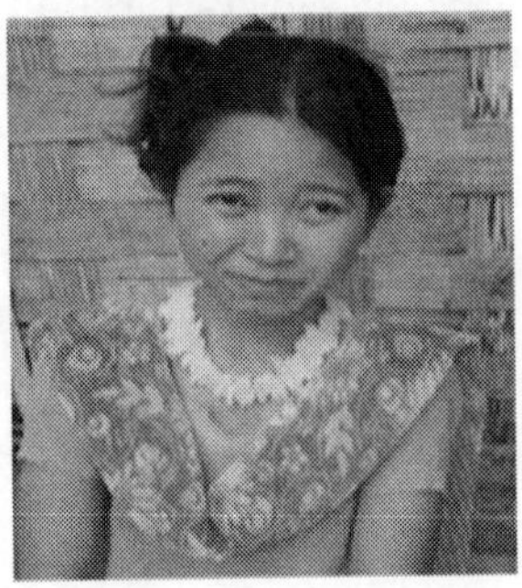

Fig. 5.5: A garland plant parts worn around the neck to cure jaundice.

Jaundice: Jaundice is treated through oral charms along with the application of herbal medicines, while some medicine man treats the disease by prescribing local medicines either in the form of syrup or plant parts to wear them on the neck or tied around the arm (Fig. 5.5). For this, roots of *Carica papaya* L. (family Caricaceae); and roots of *Musa paradisica* L. (family Musaceae) are often used. In some cases, a mixture of mustard oil and water is taken on a brass plate and placed overhead of the patient and is stirred using a heap of *Cynodon dactylon* Pers. (family Poaceae). While the medicine men or women chant charms.

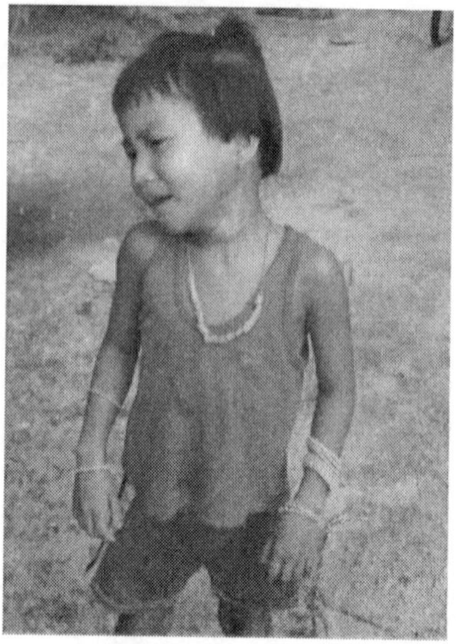

Fig. 5.6: Garland made from rhizomes of *Acorus calamus* for treatment of constipation

Constipation: Karbis adopts various practices to overcome this ailment. In one case, *Citrus* sp.; (family Rutaceae) leaf is massaged externally on belly. While in other, aroma therapy by using the rhizomes of *Acorus calamus* L. (family Araceae) is practiced where the small pieces of rhizomes are tied around the waist or neck by a thread (Fig. 5.6). Another practice is also prominent among them, where salt and betel vine is consumed for quick recovery.

Dysentery: Decoctions of the bark of *Bengvoi* (*Wrightia arborea* Dennst.; family Apocynaceae), bark of *Takarithelu* or *Phyllanthus acidus* Skeels (family Euphorbiaceae), tender leaves of *Soprim* or *Psidium gaujava* L.(family Myrtaceae), and tender leaves of *thekek* or *Cajanus cajan* L. (family Papilionaceae) are given to the patient. It is believed that the barks of both *P. acidus* and *W. arborea* are cut in an inverted position. In another form of treatment a very small amount of *Kani* or Opium (*Papaver somniferum* L.; family Papaveraceae) is stuffed in ripe banana and then given to the patient. Paste of tender shoots of *Serrata* or *Serrata chirayita* Roxb. Ex Flam. (family Gentianaceae) is also prescribed during dysentery. Leaves of *Tungmeng* or *Citrus* sp. L. (family Rutaceae) are crushed and externally applied over the abdomen of a child suffering from stomach disorder.

Diarrhoea: In case of diarrhoea, highly concentrated locally prepared rice (*Oryza sativa* L.; family Poaceae) beer or *hor lang* (*ca* 1/2 tea spoon full) is given to the child. This practice is still vibrant in rural Karbi villages.

Filarial worm: Peels of banana, seed rind of *Chuphe* or *Phaseolus aureus* Roxb. (family Leguminosae) and tender shoot of bamboo are burnt into ashes and small quantity of its ash, are mix in water and is given to the patients suffering from filarial worm.

Sleeplessness/ajo a tisso or ke-isojo: Sleeplessness is a common ailment of children during 1-4 years. Sleeplessness is said to be caused by evil spirit and the mother/elders burn eri or *Philosomia ricini* Hutt. (family Saturnidae) cocoon or cloth/cotton fibres and apply the ash on the child's head and shoulder. Garlic or *Allium sativum* L. (family Liliaceae) and charmed ginger or *Zingiber officinale* Rosc. (family Zingiberaceae) is regularly carried while travelling as it is believed to keep evil spirit at bay when a child is introduced to a new place. Besides, in order to nullify its actions, the mothers usually take six pieces of charcoal (in case of boy child) and places three of them overhead and three underfoot. In case of girls five pieces of charcoal is taken and three is kept overhead and two underfoot. The seeds of *Jangmu* or *Brassica campestries* L. (family Brassicaceae) are also sprinkled in and around the house or kept inside the pillow of children to ward off evil spirit. These above practises are still vibrant among the Karbis irrespective of economic and social status.

Cotton fibres or *Gossipium herbaceum* L. (family Malvaceae) are burnt and the ashes (*Phelo*), are applied on the body. This indigenous practice is done to drive away evil spirit and is prevalent even among the literate society.

Rabies: When a child is bitten by a dog the medicine men rolls *hilong arbi* (vermicast) over the wound and utter charms. This indigenous practice is continued for three consecutive days and herbal medicine is given on the third day. The herbal preparations involve mixing of jaggery, fresh milk with grounded roots of *Mimosa pudica* Linn. (family Mimosaceae).

Cuts and wounds: Wound due to cut is cured through oral charms followed by spitting on the wound by the medicine men. The spit of the charmer is said to give a cooling effect on the wound resulting in fast healing. Juice of petiole of *Hen* (*Arum* sp. L.; family Araceae) is said to often apply on fresh cut to stop bleeding and to cure the wound. Paste of rhizome of *Tharmit* (*Curcuma longa* L.; family Zingiberaceae) is also applied on wounds for its fast recovery.

Eye infection/sore eyes: This ailment is also cured through oral charms. The charmer, while chanting blow slowly on the infected eye. This practice is continued for six successive days (in case of boys) and five days (in case of girls).

Itchy toe and finger's gap: Ringworm in toe and finger's gap, caused due to fungal infection are claimed to be cured through oral charms followed by spitting on the wound; thereby healing the infection. Often heat is applied to cure toe infection; petiole of banana or twig of *bonbera* or *Jatropha curcas* L. (family Euphorbiaceae) is fed to fire and then applied on infected toe.

Allergy: This may be caused due to caterpillar's hair and its treatment involved oral charming and rubbing the infected part with comb or sickle (Fig. 5.7).

Insect bites: Insect stings (spider or bee) are cured through oral charms. For centipede/millipede/snake bites, fine root of *Mirabilis jalapa* L. (family Nyctaginaceae) are grounded and its paste is applied on the affected area and tied using a cotton cloth.

Women's Specific Role in Primary Healthcare

The role of women in primary healthcare is vital and at times eclipses that of men. Their involvement is not limited to healthcare but in various spheres of intangible cultural heritage such as language, codes of ethics, behavioural patterns, value systems and religious beliefs. Women are also custodians of intangible cultural heritage which encompasses, among other forms, the performing arts including music, culinary and

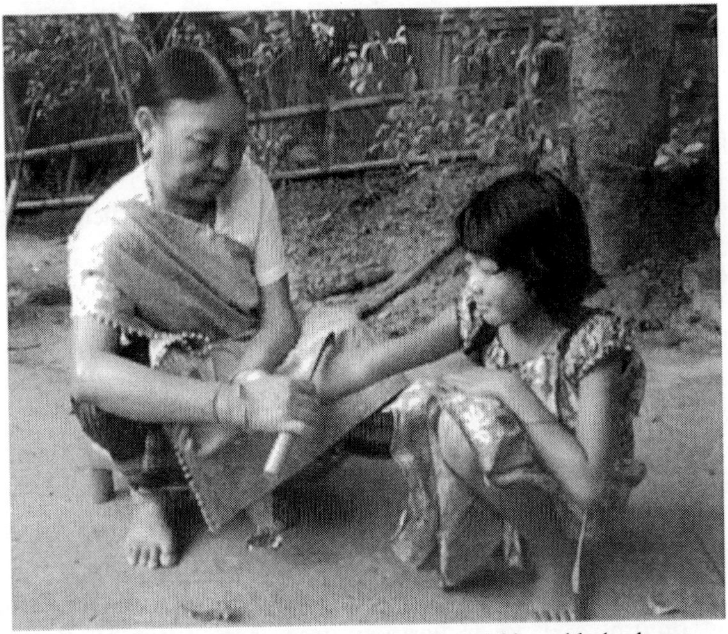

Fig. 5.7: A woman treats caterpillar allergy using sickle and holy charms.

medicinal knowledge and the know-how for the creation of material culture. Women thus, not only contribute towards healthcare but form a vital medium for transmission of cultural knowledge from one generation to another. Women-centric role in Karbi society is briefly discussed here.

Birth Attendants

Birth attendants are mostly elderly menopause women with vast knowledge and having great experience about women's health. Their service is indispensable in rural areas even today. From the time a child is expected (based on symptoms familiar to family elders), the in-laws of the pregnant woman informs birth attendants along with the female neighbours and relatives. Birth attendants perform certain rituals and based on their experiences ensure smooth delivery of the baby. From the time the mother experiences labour pain upto cutting of umbilical cord and disposal of amniotic sac, it is the exclusive domain of birth attendants, who as mentioned above are elderly menopause women. Those women who are in practice of such act is prohibited to prepare *Hor Kangthir* (holy rice beer used in rituals), as amniotic sac with its content and umbilical cord is considered impure. For the same reason, priests keep away from such activity.

Funeral Rights

Karbis perform funeral rites of a person which is performed exclusively by women. After death, the *karjong* or soul of the deceased makes a journey to *Chom arong* (i.e. the abode of Yama) where the soul is said to stay till he or she takes rebirth. Divine women singers called *Lunsepi* or *Cherhepi* through their funeral songs request the soul of the deceased to leave the earth for the *Chom arong* as he/she has been called by the Almighty. The women further request the soul not to keep any bad memories during his lifetime and not to harm any members of the family and relatives and leave in peace. If the funeral rites are not performed in the proper way it is believed that the soul remains on the earth even after cremation and in the long run will haunt the family. It may be mentioned that funeral songs are forbidden on other occasions so interested women gather in the funeral ceremony to learn from *Lunsepi* the associated funeral songs (Fig. 5.8). This case suggests the vital role of women in household well-being and women centric transmission of cultural knowledge.

Karbis also observe elaborate ritual for ultimate divinity of the deceased souls. Referred as *Chomkan*, it is the most significant and expensive religious festival of the Karbis. The festival touches upon their religion, worldviews, traditional institutions and socio-cultural life of the people. The concept of Chomkan is based on their religious worldview that after death the *karjong* do not reach *Chom arong* (the abode of king *Yama*, the god of Death) in heaven but remain as common subjects of *Chom Recho* (king Yama) and an elaborate purification ceremony is mandatory for journey to *Chom arong* (Lyall, 1908, Bordoloi, 1982). During *Chomkan*

Fig. 5.8: *Lunsepi* (second from left) sings funeral songs on the death of a person while other women listen

deceased members are called back from *Chom arong* and treated as living members by infusing lives in straw effigies. During their life they are said to fall ill and die even after providing best available treatment. The deceased are then given the same funeral rites as in the actual death and then cremated. A goat is sacrificed in honour of the most senior deceased member, the sacrifice being strictly performed by the maternal uncle of the latter. The various events and steps of *Chomkan* are narrated through folk songs by the expert *Lunsepi* or *Cherhepi* and her assistants such as *Uchepi* and *Obokpi* all women. During the festival people make merry and dance to the tune of traditional music. *Jambili Athon*, the traditional woodcraft of the Karbis is displayed by the host and participating villages on the third and final day of the festival (Teron, 2008). *Chomkan* also called *karhi* is actually an act of purification of souls; by performing *Chomkan* the family is said to be blessed by the deceased in all respects. Faulty observation of the various stages of Chomangkan festival is said to invite the wrath of the deceased members and the family will be harmed, it is believed.

Further, it is mandatory on the part of the participating villages to narrate the origin of *Jambili Athon* and its cultural significance. Men and women gather at the base of the craft and *Lunsepi* who is always a woman, sing the folk songs relating to the origin of *Jambili Athon*. It is forbidden to sing this song in day-to-day life.

During invoking of *Arnam Kethe* or the Supreme deity and *Peng* deity certain task is exclusively assigned to women. Rice beer to be used during the ritual is prepared usually by married women. On the day of the ritual, the fermented rice (as prepared above) is mixed with water and then filtered with sieves to produce a milky nutritious alcoholic drink called *Horpoh* and the process of production is called *hor kebeh*; no male can replace this task. The responsibility of drawing well water is accomplished by spinsters. On the occasion, maternal uncle, sister and neice of the host have to carry rice beer filled in *Bongkrok* (gourd shell) which is placed in *Hor-hak* (bamboo basket) and carried by women only. These are only few examples of women's specific task in the society and the list is not exhaustive. In the above discussed cases, there is no overlapping of responsibilities with male; any deviation of these social norms is considered an offence and the offender is punished as per customary law called *Adai*, the least desired treatment in the society.

Conclusion

Traditional medicines involving use of plants and animals, rituals and divination based on religious worldviews are prevalent among the Karbis as a source of primary healthcare. Traditional practices are more intense in places where access to modern medicines and medical facilities are not well established. Birth attendants still play a major role in women healthcare among rural Karbis. Some of the medicinal plants used by the Karbi tribes were also used by other tribal groups of Karbi Anglong district, Assam. For example; *Cynodon dactylon* L. is used for jaundice by the Adivasi and Boro tribes; the seeds of *Brassica campestries* L. is also used by Boro tribes for driving evil spirits. Similarly, the aroma therapeutic use of *Carica papaya* and *Musa* sp. for treatment of jaundice is also common among the Boro tribes. The use of *Allium sativa* L. and Zingiber *officinale* Rosc. has also been reported from the Adivasis, Boro and Dimasa for treatment of cough and cold in children.

Traditional healthcare practice though may not satisfy modern principles of science, it is an invaluable local knowledge system developed as a result of human interactions with nature, their beliefs, myths and religious practices. The present generation, however, hardly shows sign of inclinations to learn and preserve traditional practices and culture. Traditional knowledge is too valuable to be easily forgotten and its contribution towards human welfare has been felt across the globe. Many valuable lifesaving drugs such as *Reserpine, Codeine, Quinine, Vinblastine* and other novel drugs use today has been discovered based on traditional medicine. Proper documentation and identification of active principles of traditional medicines needs to be expedited owing to current trend of loss of biodiversity and before the knowledge holders dies.

Acknowledgement: Authors are thankful to all women informants for sharing their valuable knowledge and experiences. We also thank village elders for allowing us to attend rituals and open discussions and also local guides for guidance and hospitability.

References

Das, A.K., B.K. Dutta and G.D. Sharma (2008). Medicinal plants used by different tribes of Cachar district, Assam. *Indian Journal of Traditional Knowledge*, 7(3): 446-454.

Jain, S.K. (1988). *A Manual of Ethnobotany*, 2nd edition, Scientific Publishers (India), Jodhpur.

Jain, S.P. and J. Singh (2010). Traditional medicinal practice among the tribal people of Raigarh (Chhattisgarh), India. *Indian Journal of Natural Product and Resources*, 1(1): 109-115.

Medicinal and Aromatic plants of Assam, with special reference to Karbi Anglong, Department of Forest and Environment, Diphu.

Pandey, K. and S. Pandey (2010). Indigenous medicines of Raji Tribes of Uttarakhand. *Indian Journal of Traditional Knowledge*, 9(1):131-133.

Pattanik, C., C.S. Reddy, R. Das and P.M. Reddy (2007). Traditional Medicinal practices among the tribal people of Malkangiri district, Orissa India. *Natural Product Radiance*, 6(5):430-435.

Sajem, A.L. and K. Gosai (2010). Ethnobotanical investigation among the Lushai tribes in North Cachar hills district of Assam, North East India. *Indian Journal of Traditional Knowledge*, 9(1):108-113.

Sajem, A.L. and Gosai, K. (2006). Traditional use of medicinal plants by the Jaintia tribes in North Cachar hills district of Assam, North-East India. *J. Ethnobiol Ethnomed.*

Shankar, R., S. Dev and B.K. Sharma (2009). Traditional Healing Practices in North East India. *Current Science*, 97(1).

Sharma, N.H., P. Goswami, D. Soki, A. Jaishi and M. Das (2009) Traditional healthcare practice among the Tagin tribes of Arunachal Pradesh. *Indian Journal of Traditional Knowledge*, 8(1):127-130.

Teron, R. and P. Gogoi (2004) Indigenous means of communication amongst Social Dignitaries of Hills Karbi of Assam. *Indian Journal of Traditional Knowledge*, 3(3): 294-298.

Teron, R., R. Terangpi and U. Phangchopi (2011) Studies of Indigenous healthcare practices during pregnancy among the Karbis of North-Eastern India. *Tribal Studies*, 1:171-184.

Traditional Medicine Strategy (2002-2005). Geneva: World Health Organisation; 2002:7. http:www.who.int/medicines/library/trm/trm_str_eng.pdf

Trivedi, P.C. (2006). *Medicinal Plants: Ethnobotanical Approach,* published by Updesh Purohit for Agrobios (India), Jodhpur.

6
Health of Pre-adolescent Sonowal Kacharis of Dibrugarh District, Assam

Jaswant Singh

Introduction

Growth studies among the children have always occupied a very prominent position in the scientific research curriculum and have always received serious attention of the researchers engaged in the field of both medical science and physical anthropology all over the world (Sharma, 1970). Nutritional status is defined as the physical expression of the relationship between the nutrient intake, or bio-availability of nutrients, and the physiological requirement of an individual (Brown, 1984). Anthropometry is a widely accepted tool for assessing the nutritional status of children. Anthropometry, particularly the height and weight, are widely accepted, well documented (WHO, 1995), simple and reliable means of assessing the nutritional status of children than the time consuming and expensive biochemical test. It provides information on the past nutritional history and is an easy technique to be applied on a large size population (Johnston, 1981). Body mass index is a good indicator of current nutritional status, wasting indicates the deficiency in tissue and fat mass compared to the amount expected in a child of the same height and may have resulted either from failure to gain weight or from and may have resulted either from failure to gain weight or from actual weight loss and stunting indicates slowing in skeletal growth.

Very few nutritional anthropometric studies have been done in the State of Assam (Choudhury and Bhuyan, 1994; Choudhury *et al.,* 1995; Begum, 1996; Begum and Choudhury, 1996). All these studies reveal that a good majority of the children of the region suffers from various forms of malnutrition.

In the present study, an attempt has been made to assess the nutritional status of the Sonowal Kachari childrens belonging to pre-adolescent period from Dibrugarh district, upper Assam on the basis of anthropometric measurement and indices.

The Sonowals is enlisted as a Scheduled Tribe in the plains of Assam. They are one of the branches of the Kachari tribes of Assam, the others being Boro, Dimasa, Thengal, Mech, Semsa, Barman, Hojai, Saraniya, etc. They are mainly agriculturists and are concentrated in Dibrugarh, Tinsukia, Sibsagar, Jorhat, Golaghat, and North Lakhimpur districts of upper Assam. They had their own dialect, but at present, they have adopted Assamese language as their mother-tongue.

Materials and Method

The present study is based on a cross-sectional sample of 513 children (Boys = 256, Girls = 257) aged 6-10 years from the Sonowal Kacharis of Dibrugarh district, Assam. The anthropometric measurements recorded were height, weight and triceps skinfold following standard procedure (Cameron, 1984; Weiner and Lourie, 1981). Height of children was recorded with the help of anthropometer to the nearest 0.1 cm. The weight of the children was recorded with children wearing minimum clothing using a portable weighing scale to the nearest 0.5 kg. Skin fold measurement on triceps was taken using a Harpenden-Caliper. Data on age were based on school records and birth certificates given by the parents. However, individuals with doubtful age were excluded from the study.

Fat mass is calculated according to the formula (Sen, 1979):

$$\text{Body Fat} = \{\text{Per cent Fat} \times \text{Body Weight (kg)}\}/100$$

where,

$$\text{Per cent Fat} = (4.201/D - 3.813) \times 100$$

where,

$$D = 1.0890 - \{0.0028 \times \text{Triceps skinfold (mm)}\}$$

$$D = \text{Density}$$

And Lean Body Mass or Fat Free Mass is derived by subtracting Body Fat from Body Weight (Durnin and Womersley, 1974).

For assessing the health status of children, we have adopted three anthropometric indices—weight for age, height for age and body mass index for age, which are considered as good indicators of nutritional status. These indices were derived as Z-scores (as recommended by WHO, 1986) of the International standards or references, i.e. the growth references of the U.S. National Centre for Health Statistics (NCHS; Kuczarski *et al.*, 2000). The children were then categorized into three levels of nutritional status, following the cut-off points proposed by Visweswara Rao (1996).

Results and Discussion

The means with standard deviation of body weight, stature, triceps and body fat for both boys and girls against their age groups are shown in Table 6.1.

Weight

There is a gradual increase in average weight for both the Sonowal Kachari boys and girls from 6 years to 10 years. It is further observed that girls are slightly heavier than the boys at 7 and 10 years of age. The rate of growth per year of girls is more than the boys except at 8 years of age. They also attain maturity level earlier than boys. The boys have 29.41 per cent of mature weight (weight at 20 years of age; Singh, 2008) at 6 years of age while in the girls it is 29.55 per cent of mature level. The girls attain again around 50.00 per cent of the mature weight at 10 years of age while the boys gain only 47.71 per cent of the mature weight in the same age category.

Stature

The mean values show a gradual increase from 6-10 years of age in both Sonowal Kachari boys and girls. The differences between the mean age groups, however, suggest that the increments are not uniform over the whole period. The Sonowal Kachari boys are taller than the girls at ages 6 to 9 years, whereas the latter are taller than the former at 10 years of age but these differences are not statistically significant. It is observed that the velocity rate is more or less similar for both boys and girls at 7 and 9 years of age while in girls it is higher in 8 and 10 years. The girls approach the maturity height relatively faster than that of boys. It is observed in all the age groups. The girls attained almost 85.00 per cent of the mature height (height at 20 years) by the end of 10th year of life while the boys in that age attain 79.00 per cent of the mature height.

Triceps

The fat accumulation at triceps is greater in girls than in boys from the initial age of 6 years until the age of 10 years. It is also found that except at 8 years of age, the sex differences are statistically significant across ages. The ultimate size achieved at 10 years of age is only 6.59 mm in case of boys against 8.90 mm in case of girls. The rate of growth per year depicts higher acceleration in the Sonowal Kachari girls, barring the age group of 8 years. The boys show growth deceleration at age group of 7 to 9 years while girls show growth deceleration at age group of 8 years. Thus, the results on fat fold at triceps are inconsistent when compared with other measurements described so far.

Table 6.1: Statistical constants of weight, stature, Tricep Skinfold and Body Fat of Sonowal Kachari boys and girls

Age (Yrs)	*N*	*Weight (Kg)*		*Stature (Cm)*		*Tricep Skinfold (mm)*		*Body Fat (Kg)*		*% of Body Weight*
		$\bar{X}$	SD	$\bar{X}$	SD	$\bar{X}$	SD	$\bar{X}$	SD	
Boys			s							
6	50	16.17	1.46	106.66	3.87	7.19	1.32	1.90	0.30	11.75
7	55	18.71	1.97	114.58	4.74	6.62	1.39	2.08	0.36	11.11
8	51	20.67	2.61	119.93	5.47	6.59	1.62	2.31	0.51	11.17
9	50	23.90	3.04	126.12	6.26	6.11	1.37	2.54	0.49	10.62
10	50	26.23	3.33	131.32	4.78	6.59	2.30	2.95	1.02	11.24
Girls										
6	50	15.51	1.70	105.96	5.01	7.81	1.69	1.92	0.40	12.37
7	51	18.74	2.10	113.84	4.05	8.08	2.05	2.38	0.55	12.70
8	53	20.18	2.65	119.77	5.57	7.19	1.79	2.39	0.59	11.83
9	50	23.73	3.68	126.03	6.63	8.24	2.49	3.09	1.04	13.02
10	53	26.25	3.17	132.45	5.27	8.90	2.17	3.58	0.91	13.63

Body Fat

Statistical constants of body fat of the boys and girls against age reveals that body fat in girls is more than boys in all ages and it is statistically significant at 7 and 9 years. Among the boys body fat is 1.9 kg in the initial age of 6 years. It gradually increases and reaches 2.95 kg at 10 years. Similarly, in the girls at age 6 years body fat is 1.92 kg. It increases rapidly with the increase of age, and finally reaches 3.58 kg at 10 years. The percentage of body weight formed by fat is also higher in girls in all age groups which varies from 11.83 per cent to 13.63 per cent and that of boys varies from 10.62 per cent to 11.75 per cent.

In order to have a better understanding of the growth status of Sonowal Kachari children of the present study, an attempt has also been made to compare their weight and height with the data reported by the United States National Centre for Health Statistics (NCHS, 2000), Indian Council of Medical Research (ICMR, 1972) and pooled data of Assam (Department of Women and Child Development, Ministry of Human Resource Development, Government of India, 1998) and also with Rabha

(Choudhury, 1979) of Assam; Khynriam Khasi (Mukherjee, 2002) and War Khasi (Khongsdier, 1995) of Meghalaya.

Weight

The mean values of body weight for the Sonowal Kachari boys in comparison with Assamese, Indian and NCHS references and Rabha, Khynriam Khasi and War Khasi are shown in Table 6.5. It is seen from Table 6.5 that the Sonowal Kachari boys are lighter than the pooled data of Assamese boys from 6 to 10 years of age. They are much above the Indian boys in all the age groups. In comparison with the NCHS growth references, the Sonowal Kachari boys are below the 10th percentile from 6 to 8 years of age, and thereafter they are above the 10th percentile and below the 25th percentile of NCHS growth references. In comparison with their counterparts reported from some other population groups of North East India, the Sonowal Kachari boys are found to be heavier than the Rabha, Khynriam Khasi and War Khasi boys in the higher age groups, *i.e.*, from 10, 7, and 9 years onwards respectively. Thus, the Sonowal Kachari boys seem to be better in growth status in respect of weight when compared with Indian boys and those reported for some other population groups of North East India particularly in the higher age groups.

With regard to girls, the Sonowal Kachari girls are lighter than the Assamese girls from 6 to 10 years of age. They are heavier than the Indian girls reported by ICMR (1972) from the initial age group of 6 years to the age of 10 years. In comparison with NCHS reference, the Sonowal Kachari girls are below the 10th percentile from 6 to 8 years of age while in the rest of the age groups it is between 10th and 25th percentile. Rabha girls are heavier than the Sonowal Kachari girls from 6 to 10 years while Khynriam Khasi girls of Meghalaya are heavier at 6 and 8 years and War Khasi girls up to 8 years of age.

Stature

When Sonowal Kachari boys are compared with the pooled data

Table 6.2: Nutritional Status according to Weight for Age

Age in Years	Boys						Girls					
	≥ -2 Z Score		-2 to -3 Z		≤ -3 Z Score		≥ -2 Z Score		-2 to -3 Z		≤ -3 Z Score	
	N	%	N	%	N	%	N	%	N	%	N	%
6	20	40.00	27	54.00	3	6.00	25	50.00	12	24.00	13	26.00
7	38	69.09	9	16.36	8	14.55	37	72.55	10	19.61	4	7.84
8	34	66.67	13	25.49	4	7.84	28	52.83	7	13.21	18	33.96
9	41	82.00	6	12.00	3	6.00	32	64.00	18	36.00	0	0.00
10	41	82.00	8	16.00	1	2.00	43	81.13	10	18.87	0	0.00
6-10	174	67.97	63	24.61	19	7.42	165	64.20	57	22.18	35	13.62

$\chi^2 = 5.27$, d.f = 2

Note: ★ indicates probability level < 0.05; ≥ –2 Z Score = Normal, –2 to -3 Z Score = Moderate, ≤ –3 Z Score = Severe underweight.

Table 6.3: Nutritional Status according to Height for Age

Age in Years	Boys						Girls					
	≥ -2 Z Score		-2 to -3 Z		≤ -3 Z Score		≥ -2 Z Score		-2 to -3 Z		≤ -3 Z Score	
	N	%	N	%	N	%	N	%	N	%	N	%
6	31	62.00	14	28.00	5	10.00	29	58.00	11	22.00	10	20.00
7	40	72.73	11	20.00	4	7.27	33	64.71	14	27.45	4	7.84
8	42	82.36	8	15.68	1	1.96	34	64.15	14	26.42	5	9.43
9	40	80.00	9	18.00	1	2.00	32	64.00	14	28.00	4	8.00
10	47	94.00	3	6.00	0	0.00	46	86.79	6	11.32	1	1.89
6-10	200	78.12	45	17.58	11	4.30	174	67.70	59	22.96	24	9.34

$\chi^2 = 8.52$ ⋆, d.f = 2

Note: ⋆ indicates probability level < 0.05; ≥ -2 Z Score = Normal; -2 to -3 Z Score = Moderate; < -3 Z Score = Severely stunted.

Table 6.4: Nutritional Status according to Body Mass Index for Age

Age in Years	Boys						Girls					
	≥ - 2 Z Score		–2 to –3 Z		≤ –3 Z core		≥ –2 Z Score		–2 to –3 Z		≤ –3 Z Score	
	N	%	N	%	N	%	N	%	N	%	N	%
6	40	80.00	6	12.00	4	8.00	39	78.00	7	14.00	4	8.00
7	41	74.55	11	20.00	3	5.45	46	90.20	5	9.80	0	0.00
8	41	80.39	8	15.69	2	3.92	41	77.36	11	20.75	1	1.89
9	45	90.00	4	8.00	1	2.00	46	52.00	4	8.00	0	0.00
10	44	88.00	3	6.00	3	6.00	45	84.91	7	13.21	1	1.89
6-10	211	82.42	32	12.50	13	5.08	217	84.44	34	13.23	6	2.33

$\chi^2 = 2.72$, d.f = 2

Note: ⋆ indicates probability level < 0.05; ≥ –2 Z Score = Normal; –2 to –3 Z Score = Moderate; ≤ –3 Z Score = Severely wasted

Table 6.5: Comparison of Weight (kg) of Sonowal Kachari with that of Assamese, Indian and NCHS references and neighbouring tribes

Age (in years)	*Assam (Pooled)*	*Indian (ICMR)*	*NCHS 10th*	*Present Study*	*Rabha*	*Khynriam Khasi*	*War Khasi*
Boys							
6	17.20	15.90	17.49	16.17	17.93	17.10	17.83
7	19.20	17.60	19.38	18.71	20.17	18.11	19.69
8	21.50	19.30	21.40	20.67	21.59	20.65	21.25
9	24.50	21.10	23.57	23.90	23.96	23.04	23.48
10	27.10	23.10	25.99	26.23	25.70	24.59	25.40
Girls							
6	17.00	15.40	16.98	15.51	16.81	17.74	17.00
7	18.80	17.20	18.89	18.73	19.07	18.69	18.82
8	21.40	18.80	20.96	20.19	20.97	20.41	20.27
9	24.30	20.80	23.32	23.73	24.50	22.68	22.65
10	26.60	22.50	26.08	26.25	26.51	24.72	24.74

Table 6.6: Comparison of Stature (cm) of Sonowal Kachari with that of Assamese, Indian & NCHS reference & neighbouring tribes

Age (in years)	*Assam (Pooled)*	*Indian (ICMR)*	*NCHS 10th*	*Present Study*	*Rabha*	*Khynriam Khasi*	*War Khasi*
Boys							
6	109.00	107.40	108.66	106.66	110.15	103.21	107.98
7	115.10	113.20	114.64	114.58	116.97	108.69	113.86
8	120.80	118.60	120.37	119.93	120.08	113.61	118.96
9	125.70	123.00	125.54	126.12	125.98	119.20	124.20
10	130.70	128.10	130.11	131.32	129.86	122.76	127.52
Girls							
6	109.00	106.30	108.05	105.96	109.78	103.43	107.24
7	114.80	111.90	114.40	113.78	115.17	108.65	111.23
8	120.70	117.20	120.09	119.86	119.91	114.19	116.02
9	125.70	122.20	124.97	126.03	127.40	118.87	121.27
10	130.60	126.70	129.39	132.67	131.77	122.63	127.15

of Assamese, Indian and NCHS references (Table 6.6), it is found that the Sonowal Kachari boys are taller than the Assamese boys from 9 years onwards and Indian boys in almost all the age groups. However, it is below the 10th percentile of NCHS reference from 6 to 8 years and in the rest of the age groups it is between the 10th and 25th percentile. Table clearly shows that the Sonowal Kachari boys are taller than the Khynriam Khasi and War Khasi boys throughout the age groups and with Rabha boys, they are taller in 9 and 10 years.

As for the Sonowal Kachari girls, they lie below the 10th percentile of the NCHS growth references from 6 to 8 years of age, and thereafter it moves above the 10th percentile. In comparison with the Assamese (pooled) data and the data reported by ICMR (1972) on girls of India, Table 6.6 shows that like the boys, in case of girls too, except at age group of 6 to 8 years in case of pooled Assamese girls and at 6 years of age in case of Indian girls reported by ICMR (1972), the Sonowal Kachari girls are taller. Compared with the other population groups of North East India the Sonowal Kachari girls are much taller than the Khynriam Khasi and War Khasi. However, the Sonowal Kachari girls are shorter than the Rabha girls at age group of 6 to 9 years.

In the present study, we have taken three important anthropometric indices, that is, weight for age, height for age and body mass index for age for assessing the nutritional status of the Sonowal Kachari children which are shown in Tables 6.2, 6.3 and 6.4 respectively for both Sonowal Kachari boys and girls.

Weight for Age

Table 6.2 shows that in the age group of 6 to 10 years of age, 24.61 per cent and 7.42 per cent of boys and 22.18 per cent and 13.62 per cent of girls are in the categories of moderate and severe forms of under weight, respectively. Thus, it indicates that the prevalence of under nutrition is slightly higher in the Sonowal Kachari girls than in boys in pre adolescent age group. However, the difference is not statistically significant ($\chi^2 = 5.27$, df = 2, P > 0.05). Incidence of the normal weight for age gradually increases while frequency of moderate and severely wasted decreases along with the increase in age for both boys and girls.

Besides sex variation in the distribution of low weight for age as mentioned above, Table 6.2 further shows that the frequencies of under weight (i.e. moderate plus severe forms) in the Sonowal Kachari boys and girls for the age groups 6 to 10 years are 32.03 per cent, and 35.80 per cent respectively.

Height for Age

Table 6.3 shows the percentage distribution of growth retardation in the Sonowal Kachari boys and girls. It is observed that about 78 per cent of boys and 67 per cent of girls falls in the normal category. The frequencies of moderate and severe forms of stunting growth retardation in boys are about 17.58 per cent and 4.30 per cent respectively, where as in girls these frequencies are found to be about 22.96 per cent and 9.34 per cent respectively. Thus, the prevalence of stunting in pre-adolescent age group is significantly higher in girls than in boys ($\chi^2 = 8.52$, df = 2, P < 0.05). It is also observed that children in the lower age group record higher incidence of low height for age as compared to those in higher age group.

Body Mass Index for Age

Body Mass Index (BMI) is generally considered as the best indicator of body fat mass, or thinness due to Chronic Energy Deficiency (Ferro-Luzi *et al.*, 1992; WHO, 1995). Considering all age groups, Table 6.4 shows that 82.42 per cent of Sonowal Kachari boys and 84.44 per cent of girls are in the normal grade of nutritional status. In other words, the frequencies of moderate and severe grades of CED in boys are about 12.5 per cent and 5.08 per cent respectively. While in girls, these frequencies are about 13.23 per cent and 2.33 per cent respectively. Thus, the prevalence of CED is relatively higher in the Sonowal Kachari boys (17.58%) than in girls (15.56%), and the variation observed is statistically non-significant ($\chi^2 = 2.72$, d.f = 2, $P < 0.05$).

To sum up our description of the anthropometric indices to assess nutritional status, it is found that the prevalence of under nutrition in both Sonowal Kachari boys and girls for all age groups is higher in weight for age (33.92%) and height for age (27.10%) when compared with that indicated by BMI (16.57%). It seems that the present population under study is high in terms of the severity of under nutrition, according to the classificatory criteria proposed by Gorstein *et al.* (1994).

References

Begum, G., (1996). Health status of school children of Guwahati city. pp. 128-143. In *Communities of North East India.* F.A. Das and I. Barua (Eds). Mittal Publications, New Delhi.

Begum, G. and Choudhury, B., (1996). A nutritional surveillance among the Assamese Muslim of Kamrup District Assam. *Ind. Anthrop.*, 26, 1: 1-25.

Brown, K.H., (1984). Measurements of dietary intake. *Population Development Review* (Suppl) 10: 69-91.

Cameron, N. (1984). *The Measurement of Human Growth*. Sydney, Australia. Croom Helm Ltd.

Choudhury, B. (1979). *A Cross Sectional Study of Growth of Some Somatometric Characters of Rabha Boys of Kamrup District, Assam.* Unpublished Ph.D. Thesis, Gauhati University.

Choudhury, B. and Bhuyan, S.C., (1994). Growth and nutritional status of Kalita children of Kamrup district, Assam. *Bull. Deptt. Anthrop.* Gauhati. University, 8: 65-86.

Choudhury, B., Begum, G., and Barua, T., (1995). Nutritional status of school going children of Guwahati City. *Bull. Deptt. Anthrop.* Gauhati University, 9: 122-134.

Durnin, J.V.G.A. and Womersley, J. (1974). Body fat assessed from total body density and its estimation from Skinfold thickness: Measurements on 481 men and women aged 16 to 72 years. *British Journal of Nutrition*. 32, 77-97.

Gorstein, J., K. Sulivan, R. Yip, M. de Onis, F. Fajans and G. Clugston. (1994), Issues in the assessment of nutritional status using anthropometry. *W.H.O. Bulletin,* 72: 273-282.

Government of India. (1998). *India Nutrition Profile.* Department of Women and Child Development, Ministry of Human Resource Development, Government of India.

Indian Council of Medical Research (I.C.M.R.) (1972). Growth and Physical Development of Indian Infants and Children. *Indian Council of Medical Research Technical Report Series No. 18.* New Delhi: Indian Council of Medical Research.

Johnston, F.E., (1981). Anthropometry and Nutritional Status, in Assessing Changing Food Consumption Pattern, pp. 252-264, Committee on Food Consumption Patterns.

Khongsdier, R. (1995). *A Study on Nutrition and Health Status in Relation to Some Bio Social Factors among the War Khasi of Meghalaya.* Unpublished Ph.D. thesis, North Eastern Hill University, Shillong, Meghalaya.

Kuczmarski, R.J., C.L. Ogden, L.M., Grummer-Strawn, K.M. Flegal, S.S. Guo, R. Wei, Z. Mei, L.R. Curtin, A.F. Roche, and C.L. Johnson, (2000). Growth charts: United States. Advance data from vital and health statistics. Revised (Hyattsville, Maryland: National Centre for Health Statistics).

Mukherjee, N., (2002). *Studies on Demography and Growth Pattern among the Khasi Children of Shillong, Meghalaya.* Unpublished Ph.D. thesis, North Eastern Hill University, Shillong, Meghalaya.

National Centre for Health Statistics (N.C.H.S.), (2000). *CDC Growth Charts for the United States: Methods and Development.* Series Report 11, No. 241.

Sen, R.N. (1979). c.f. Singh, I.P. and Bhasin, M.K. (2004). *A Manual of Biological Anthropology*. Delhi, India. Kamla Raj Enterprises.

Sharma, J.C. (1970). *Physical Growth and Development of the Maharastrians.* Ethnographic and Folk Culture Society, Lucknow.

Weiner, J.S. and Lourie, J.A. (1981). Practical Human Biology, London. Academic Press.

World Health Organization (WHO) (1995), *Physical Status: The Use and Interpretation of Anthropometry*. World Health Organization, Geneva.

World Health Organization (WHO) (1986), Use and Interpretation of Anthropometric Indicators of Nutritional Status. *Bulletin of the World Health Organization,* 64: 929-941.

7
Ethnoichthyological Notes on the Use of Fish in Traditional Medicine Among the Karbis of Assam

Valentina Teronpi, A.K. Tamuli and
Robindra Teron

Introduction

Traditional medicine forms the main source of primary healthcare particularly in developing countries but its popularity in developed countries is equally important with modern medicines. It has been relied upon to support, promote, retain and regain human health for millennia. The World Health Organization (WHO) defines traditional medicine as "the sum total of knowledge, skill and practices based on theories, beliefs and experiences indigenous to different cultures that are used to maintain health, as well as to prevent, diagnose, improve or treat physical and mental illnesses." About 80 per cent of the population in some African and Asian countries are dependent on traditional medicines for primary healthcare. Use of traditional medicine is equally significant in the developed countries; 70 per cent to 80 per cent of the population has used some form of "alternative" or "complementary" medicines (WHO, 2008). Although traditional medicine mainly relies on herbal treatment, animals traditional medicine mainly relies on herbal treatment, animals or animal derived products are also used. It has been reported that more than half of the world's modern drugs are of biological resources and that of 252 that has been selected by WHO as essential to human health, 8.7 per cent come from animal sources (Marques, 1997). It is fair to say that animals have been playing a significant role in healing processes, folk rituals and religious practices of the people from all five continents.

Traditional healthcare practice or folk medicine of the Karbi community involves numerous magico-religious observations and herbal prescriptions. These local prescriptions include plants and animals or their products and also sometimes minerals. Besides other ingredients, fish form integral part of traditional medicines which are used in oral therapy as well as in rituals. Traditional knowledge of such practices is transferred orally from one generation to another by words of mouth. Karbis, belonging to the Mongoloid stock, are prominent ethnic group of Assam, distinct in their traditions and cultures. They speak local dialect of the Tibeto-Burman group particularly the Kuki-Chin sub-group of languages (Bhattacharjee, 1986; Phangcho, 2001). Karbis follow patrilineal system of family and socially divided into five major *Kur* or clans, *viz. Lijang, Hanjang, Ejang, Kronjang* and *Tungjang*. These clans are exogamous, which means marriages between members of the same clan are not allowed. Traditional religion of the Karbis is animistic which preaches immortality of souls and rebirth, while about 15 per cent Karbis are Christians (Census of India, 2011). Honoring the *terim* or ancestors and rituals are integral part of their traditional religion. Majority of the Karbis in Karbi Anglong district still practice traditional medicine in primary healthcare system. Lack of modern medical facilities, poverty and traditional culture are the main factors for continuation of traditional medicines. Further, traditional medicines are considered more effective, without side effects, than modern medicines for some diseases.

Zootherapy is an integral part of traditional healthcare system of the Karbis but only one report has been published in this regard

(Ronghang *et al.*, 2011). Among animal taxa used as medicinal sources, ichthyofauna or fish requires special attention due to their strong representation in the medicinal use and also in the religious healing practices. Although few works have been reported on the therapeutic use of ichthyofauna in India and abroad (Sakia and Ahmed, 2012; Deb and Haque, 2011; Orilogbon and Adewole, 2011 etc.), icthyofauna as a source of medicine in Karbi's folk medicine have till now received only scant attention and the present paper is an initiative to document use of fish in traditional healthcare practices.

Material and Methods

Field study was undertaken during the period from March 2011 to June 2012 among the Karbis and a few other ethnic groups in Karbi Anglong district (25° 33′ N to 26°35′ N Latitude and 92°10′ to 93°50′ E Longitude), Assam. Unstructured and structured interview methods were used for collecting information from thirty persons, randomly selected from different localities. The selection of the informants was based on their recognition as experts and knowledgeable concerning traditional healthcare practices. The informants were first apprised of the objectives. Information disclosed by informants was substantiated from elders of other localities and also by personal observations. We also attended rituals and social occasions for personal observations of fishes in healing practices. Fishes collected with the help of local guides were identified using standard literatures (Jayaram, 2001 and Vishwanath, 2002). Similar study was also undertaken among Dimasa and Thadou ethnic groups and the results compared.

Results and Discussions

Fish is primarily used as source of food and protein among the Karbis. Fish is integral part of the socio-religious life of the Karbis. Fish is also used in traditional medicine as local prescriptions and also used in rituals as part of healing practices. Use of fish to cure mental depression—like symptoms locally referred as *Nihu kachingtung* is prevalent till today among the Karbis. Studies among the Dimasa and Thadou tribes also revealed use of fishes in traditional medicine. The paper report use of 14 species of fish in the treatment of 25 disease conditions; fish with local names in Karbi, Dimasa and Thadou is tabulated (Table 7.1).

Ethnoichthyology of the Karbis

Karbis maintain close relationship with nature and its components which form the basis of mutual co- existence since time immemorial. Besides fish being an important diet in the community, there is a rich compendium of fish folklore which encompasses myths, metaphors, folktales, proverbs, songs etc. Fish is an important item in the Karbi kitchen and also supplements protein requirement. Fish items are prepared by different methods depending on resource availability and local conditions. Generally, Karbis prefer to consume fish cooked without oil. Small fish is often cooked with local spice *lopong* (*Ocimum kilimandscharicum* Guerke) to remove the unpalatable smell; sometimes *nempo* or sesame powder is added to enhance the taste of the preparation. Often fishes are roasted over fire and preserved for later use; such fish preparation is called *kephi*. For special occasion, fishes are cooked in *langpong* (bamboo tubes) and such items are highly revered.

Dried fish is one of the essential ingredients in every Karbi household as it has both social and religious significance. Sun dried small fishes are called *aiva*, smoked fish are known as *ke-ur* and fermented dried fish is referred as *menthu*. Big fishes are cut into small pieces lengthwise and smoked over the fire; this is called *toman*. The latter is consumed by roasting over fire or eaten cooked. Usually *Puntius* sp. are dried and fermented in earthen pots (then called *tibuk menthu*) or in *langpong* (then called *langpong menthu*). Fermented dried fish has strong aroma but when cooked is said to be pleasant and refreshing.

There are many cases or instances to suggest influence of

Table 7.1: Inventory of fish used for medicinal purpose by the Karbi, Dimasa and Thadou tribes in Karbi Anglong district

Sl. No.	*Scientific name*	*Local name*	*Tribe*	*Disease condition*	*Parts used and Application*
1.	*Danio aequipinnatus*	*Nune*	Karbis	Constant spitting or *ingthokset*	The whole fish is boiled and consumed regularly.
2.	*Monopterus cuchia*	*Kumchirui*	Karbis	Anaemia	Raw blood of the fish taken orally.
			Karbis	Kalazar	Small sized raw fish is taken orally or fresh blood of the fish is consumed.
			Karbis	Entry of leech	Fresh blood of the fish is consumed raw as tonic for removal of leech from rectum/anus.
		Namna	Dimasas	Weakness after delivery	Fish is boiled and taken.
3.	*Puntius* sp.	*Ok-puthi*	Karbis	Night-blindness	Cooked head of the fish is taken regularly.
			Thadous	Memory	Boiled head of the fish is taken to increase memory.
4.	*Clarius batrachus*	*Nagur*	Karbis	Small pox	Cooked fish is eaten.
		Nagen	Dimasas	Weakness after delivery	Boiled fish is taken regularly.
5.	*Mystus* sp.	*Tengera*	Karbis	Small pox	Cooked fish is eaten.
6.	Any hillstream fish		Karbis	Sore festering wounds	The affected area is bandage with fish belly and kept for 2-3 days.
7.	*Channa gachua*	*Ok-langso*	Karbis	When pricked by thorn	The bile of the fish is applied when pricked by a thorn, it becomes easy to remove.
			Dimasas	Dysentery	The fish mixed with common salt is wrapped in a banana leave and boiled and the boiled fish is taken.
8.	*Puntius* sp. (fermented)	*Manthu*	Karbis	Blood purifier	*Manthu* is cooked with bamboo shoot and taken.
				Common cold	*Manthu* is cooked with chilli and taken to cure common cold.
9.	*Anguilla bengalensis*	*Nujung*	Karbis	Rheumoid-arthritis	The fat of the fish is used as a ointment.
10.	*Heteropnues-tes fossilis*	*Singki*	Karbis	Sting by the fish itself	The brain of the fish is used as an antidote. The brain is consumed raw when stung by the fish itself.
		Nagen	Dimasas	Weakness after delivery	Boiled fish is taken.
11.	*Wallago atu*	*Seketa*	Karbis	To maintain health of the liver	Boiled head of the fish is taken regularly.
12.	*Labeo pangusia*	*Notun*	Karbis	Weakness after delivery	Boiled fish is taken regularly.
			Karbis/ Dimasas	Stomach ache	Bile of the fish is taken orally.
13.	*Channa punctatus*	*Ok-meklot/ ok-borok*	Karbis	Corn or clavus	The eyes of the fish is mixed with common salt applied to the corn affected part of the body.
		Ngavo	Thadous	Diarrhoea	Boiled fish is taken.
			Thadous	Swelling of the testicle	The head of the fish is tapped on the affected testicle.
14.		*Thinkha*	Thadous	Malaria	The bile of the fish is taken at least 3 times a day.

fish on language. Fish characters are framed into proverbs for imparting moral lessons. Karbi proverbs such as *ebi vet a-ok abeng kachingtip* which means fishes of the same pond snapping at each other's fins or *ok avete cheheta ok*, meaning, crab is better than no fish at all. Metaphorically, the former speaks of situation of infighting within a group or organization. The later explains a condition of scarcity wherein a person is compelled to be satisfied against his or her wish. Fish also has influence on the material life of the Karbis particularly women. Backbone of fish is a common a motif in *pini kamphlak* or lower garment of women, as old as the origin of the garment or costume (Teron and Borthakur, 2012). In the early Karbi society fish is considered as indicator of social status. *Toman* is considered revered commodity and offered to deities such as *Arnam Kethe* and *Hemphu* during rituals. As a parallel, a person who is honoured with *toman* is considered as having equal status with the deities *Arnam Kethe* and *Hemphu*. Behaviour of fish is often used as indicator of season change. Breeding season of the hillstream fish *nuhong* (*Garra* sp.) is used as indicator of the month march (Teron and Borthakur, 2008). Upstream migration is said to indicate the onset of rainy season or persistence of rain while downstream migration indicates end of rainy season. *Ok-kipru* or community fishing is an annual grand occasion that touches upon the traditional institutions, religion and social life of the Karbis, and therefore, showcases their cultural heritage.

Fish also occupies an important place in the traditional healthcare practices. Fishes are used to address a host of health related disorders such as cough, anemia, etc. among different tribes of Karbi Anglong district, namely Karbi, Dimasa and Thadou tribes (Table 7.1). Some fishes are avoided during certain illnesses for example among the Karbis, the patient suffering from throat problem, goitre or leprosy is barred from eating scaled fishes. Tuberculosis patients are barred from eating fishes. Similarly, among the Dimasas the patient suffering from dermis problem are barred to eat *Puntius* sp., *Wallago atu* is also avoided during illnesses and during urinary tract infection the head of the fish is avoided.

Fishing is usually done using traditional gears like hooks (*arhi*), different types of nets (*lantar, lanjong, lunvung* etc.) and different types of traps (*ru-pat, ru-krak, ru-pharlip* etc.) depending upon the size of the waterbody. *Arsan* or fishing weirs are also used for catching fishes. Apart from the fishing gears *hiru* or piscicidal plants such as *rumet* (*Derris elliptica* Benth.), *sirhoop* (*Mimosa himalayana* Gamble.), *ruteng* (*Linostoma decandrum* Wall.), *ruthe* (*Randia dumentorum* Poir.) are used for stupefying fishes, which are then caught.

Traditional Worldviews and Primary Healthcare Practices

Karbis believe in multiple gods and considers all objects on earth to possess divinity or spirits and therefore, propitiation of these spirits/deities for well-being of individuals, households and the community. Unless propitiated, these spirits may become potentially dangerous and harmful causing sicknesses, deaths, crop-failures, draught or erratic animal behaviours. Karbis worship household deities called *Hem Angtar* and these deities are propitiated annually. There are deities who are propitiated as and when required and designated as *Habit ase* (non-household gods). A disease condition is referred as *se kelong*. When a person falls ill the cause is attributed to the wrath of the deities/spirits and initiates propitiation of the deities/spirits. In such cases the household members seek the help of diviner. The diviner through divination, identifies the deity/spirit responsible for the illness and suggests certain rituals for recovery of the patient. This act of divination is called *Sang Kelang*. The practice is more prevalent in remote areas where modern medical facility is a far cry. Sickness, if long continued or severe, is frequently attributed to witchcraft (*maja*) and the patient is said to be *maja kelong*—witchcraft has got hold of him.

Traditional healthcare of the Karbis include both local and oral applications, and rituals to cure host of diseases like anemia, muscular inflammation, pain (analgesia), etc. *Keso* or illness is also called *se-kelong*, a generic term for contacting illnesses and its treatment is called *se-kelang*. *Se-kelang*, therefore, involves numerous sacred healing incantations, chants, prayers and rituals and in some cases administration of plant and animal products. The rituals may be widely divided into (a) *kapherem* and (b) *karkli*. In *kapherem*, a cure for certain *keso* (pain or illness) is sought by performing healing chants involving external application of saliva of the mouth (*kehi/kangthok*) and mild blowing of air (*kebut*) on the afflicted portion of the body. *Kapherem* is performed for the cure of numerous pains or *keso* such as *Ingki Angmi* (toxins of caterpillars), *Bap Ase*, *Ingthum* (Boils/Furuncle), *Methan Kekor* (Dog bite), *Pok Avur* (epidemic of stomach disease), *But Pharo* (Acute Stomach ache), *Chor Kedong* (Thorn inflicted injury), *Me Kapherem* (Burn), *Inghai* (lymph adinitis), *Han Kangri* (Vegetable Poisoning), *Sor Kapherem* (Acute pain), *Mek Avur* (Epidemic of eye disease), *Chainong a-But* (Acute stomach pain), *Thengkur* (Poisoning) and *Phurui Kangthok* (Snake bite) etc., to cite a few. In *kapherem*, blood-sacrifice is generally not involved. In extreme cases when the *keso* does not respond to *kapherem*, blood-sacrifice or *karkli* is resorted to. Philosophically, therefore, in traditional Karbi healing system, blood-sacrifice is not the first option.

In *karkli*, a priest resorts to reading of entrail and liver of sacrificed chickens, goats or pigs. This practice of divining, known since the time of ancient Etruscans, Romans, and the Mesopotamians is known as *haruspicy*, *hepatoscopy* or *hepatomancy*, the inspection of the entrails of sacrificed animals, especially the livers of sacrificed sheep and poultry. The practice is also known as 'Extispicy (from Latin *extispicium*), the practice of using anomalies in animal entrails to predict or divine future events. Organs inspected include the liver, intestines, and lungs. The animal used for extispicy must often be ritually pure and slaughtered in a special ceremony.' Besides the reading of the entrails and livers etc., the direction of the head and wings of the sacrificed chicken is also examined.

Ritual use of Fish

All rituals are associated with various healing practices or general well-being of individuals, household or village communities which are performed either at home, within the boundary of a village or in the woods (in a safe distance from village). Fish is symbolically used in all the healing practices. Fish (of any species) is collected from rivers (or from ponds these days) one day ahead of the ritual and brought home which is then cooked (only boiled without adding any flavour or salt). The boiled fish is then wrapped in a leaf and tied with nine strands of *jintak* (bamboo rope). This fish thus sanctified is called *beng* which is offered at the altar where the particular deities are worshipped.

Beng is used in the rituals for *Hem Angtar* or household deities such as *Peng*, *Rong Arnam*, *Chojun* and *Rongker*. In the beginning of the ritual the *Kurusar* or priest pay obedience and honour to his predecessors by offering rice beer followed by *beng*. By this practice the *kurusar* is said to inform his *kuru* or predecessors that the former is performing the ritual acquired from them and did not act unilaterally and ask for blessings for smooth conduct of the ritual. Ritual without honouring the *kuru* by the *kurusar* is said to be incomplete. *Beng* or sanctified fish is not offered at rituals generally performed in the woods called *bit-ase* such as *duikrai* or *chekama*.

During *Chojun*, the supreme deity of Karbi pantheon *Arnam Kethe* (variously known as *Barithe, Abinong*, *Athak Asor* etc.) is offered live fish or *ok-kereng* of two varieties, namely *nune* (*Amblypharyngodon mola*, *Danio aequipinnatus*) and *ok-langso* (*Channa gachua*) along with *chehe* (*Carcinus* sp.) and *kumphi* (*Dytiscus marginalis*).

Nihu Kachingtung, Mental Depression-like Condition

As a society, Karbis are organized around a network of kinship relations. The maternal uncles are held in high esteem in Karbi society and traditionally, it is customary for all sisters to pay periodic homage to their brothers. When a sister's son/daughter is afflicted with certain socially defined conditions such as biting nails, pulling one's hair, aloofness and loss of appetite (with no physical evidence of illness), the condition is said to be attributed to *Nihu kachingtung/kachiri* (*Nihu*, maternal uncle; *kachingtung/ kachiri*, longing) or the curse of maternal uncle. Often the help of a diviner is sought to determine the particular brother (elder or younger) who is to be ritually propitiated. The particular *nihu* (maternal uncle) is then approached, offered customary wine, who will then give six fist-full of rice and six pieces of *toman* (dried fish prepared out of bigger varieties of fish of any species) for the afflicted person. The quantity of ritual gift is five fist-full of rice and five pieces of *toman* if the afflicted person is female and six fist-full of rice and six pieces of *toman* if the afflicted person is male. If the person partakes the ritual gifts (of rice and *toman*), the abnormalities are said to be cured.

Conclusion

Besides food, fish is used in traditional healing practices and zootherapy still remains very prevalent particularly among rural Karbis. Due to easy availability of the fishes and limited access to modern medicine the Karbi people became dependent on this water resource for primary healthcare and day-to-day practices. Use of fish to cure mental depression like symptoms locally referred as *Nihu kachingtung* is prevalent till today irrespective of social or economic status. Dimasa and Thadou tribes also use fish in traditional medicine. Traditional healthcare a practice is a result of human interactions with his environment such practices is based on resource availability and therefore, provides information about diversity and distribution of organisms in the past. Further, traditional knowledge of indigenous people can provide leads for sustainable use and management of natural resources. Today, however, unmindful exploitation has pushed our resources towards the brink of collapse. Destructive fishing practices by poisoning water bodies with synthetic chemicals pose serious threats to aquatic fauna particularly the hillstream ecosystem. Studies should explore inclusion of traditional knowledge of local communities in framing management policies that will solve problems of the people as well as conserve natural resources.

Acknowledgement: Authors are highly indebted to informants for sharing their knowledge on traditional healthcare practices in general and fish in particular. Authors are also thankful to local guides for their help and co-operation during the field study.

References

1. World Health Organisation Fact Sheet No. 134 (December 2008). *Traditional Medicine.*
2. Marques, J.G.W. (1997). Faunal medicinal: recurso do ambiente on ameaca a biodiversidade? *Mutum*, 1(1):4.
3. Ronghang, R., Teron, R., Tamuli, A.K., and Rajkhowa, R.C. (2011). Traditional zootherapy practiced among the Karbis of Assam (India). *The Ecoscan*, 1:161-166.
4. Saikia, K. and Ahmed, R. (2012). Wetland fish diversity of Majuli river island (India) and their medicinal values. *The Clarion*, 1: 91-96.
5. Deb, K.A. and Haque, C.E. (2011). 'Every mother is a mini doctor': Ethnomedicinal use of fish, shellfish and some other aquatic animals in Bangladesh. *Journal of Ethnopharmacology*.134; pp. 259-267.
6. Orilogbon, J.O. and Adewole, A.M. (2011): Ethnoichthyological knowledge and perception in traditional medicine in Onde and Lagos states, southeast Nigeria, *Egyptian Journal of Biology*. Vol. 13; pp. 57-64.
7. Phangcho, P.C. (2001): *Karbi Anglong and North Cachar Hills: A Study of Geography and Culture*, Printwell, Diphu.
8. Bhattacharjee, T. (1986): *Sociology of the Karbis*, B.R. Publishing Corporation, Delhi.
9. Jayaram, K.C. (2001): *Freshwater fishes of Indian Region*. Narendra Publishing House, Delhi.
10. Vishwanath, W. (2002): *Fishes of North East India: a field guide to species identification*. R & K Packaging Industries, Imphal.

11. Teron, R. and Borthakur, S.K. (2012). Biological motifs and designs on traditional costumes among *Karbis* of Assam. *Indian Journal of Traditional Knowledge*. 11(2), 305-308.
12. Teron, R. and Borthakur, S.K. (2008). Traditional Knowledge relating to flora and fauna as indicators in predicting annual seasons among *Karbi* tribe of Assam. *Indian Journal of Traditional Knowledge*. 8(4), pp. 518-524.

8
Health Care Practices in Tea-Estates in Cachar District of Assam
A Sociological Study

Atuwar Rahman

Introduction

The study intends to emphasis nature of health care practice prevalent among tea-estates in Cachar district of Assam. In this scheme of presentation, I attempt to present a detail of fieldwork done during my study. For this study, eight-tea estate has been selected randomly based on direction (location) perspective. For the study, total sample size of population set as 320. The criteria sample has been taken randomly as 40 from each tea estate covering equal numbers of male and female population. The survey of related studies has been done by visiting several libraries of different colleges and universities across the state as well as reading journals and books related to sociological and public health studies. An interview schedule has been developed and used to collect data from study areas. Study material (including primary and secondary data) and review along with problem faced during data collection are designed systematically as follows—introduction, research questions, objectives of study, hypothesis, universe of study, operational definition, implications, reviews of literature and collection of secondary data, problems faced during data collection, conclusion and references.

of literature and collection of secondary data, problems faced during data collection, conclusion and references.

The study has been conducted purely to seek out answers of the following questions, *viz*. Why people of tea gardens suffer from high rate of illness and death? Is prevalent traditional health care practice directly responsible for high rate of illness and death?

Objectives of Study

The study is based on following predetermined objectives—

1. To study health care practices in tea estates of Cachar district.
2. To study cause of poor health care practices in tea estates.
3. To study implementation and impact of different health policy.

Hypothesis

Assumptions determined for the study are as follows:

1. People of the study area are conservative about religious activities like *puja-parvana* for treatment of disease.
2. Absence of modern treatment along with failure of traditional method of treatment cause more health problems for people of the study area.

Review of Literature and Collection of Secondary Source of Data

J. Rourke (2008), in his article "Rural Health in South Asia" has stated that the common leading causes of death in rural areas include higher risks of cardiovascular and respiratory diseases, as well as injury (i.e., poisonings, motor vehicle accidents). Again, further adding to the complexities of rural health, there are exceptions to the given statistics. For instance, opposite trends were found in India where urban dwellers were more likely to have been diagnosed with heart diseases, asthma, arthritis, and osteoporosis than their rural counterparts. These conflicting results confirm that much still needs to be learned regarding the impact of 'place' on health.

M.N. Srinivas (1979) in his monograph 'Management of Rural Health Care' reviews efforts of government in delivery of health care services to rural people since beginning of planned era. He says people living in interior and remote rural areas do not have access to primary health care. Problem of health care service in rural areas has peculiar characteristics like their concept of health, disease is traditional, apathy towards allopathic medical practitioners, limited capacity to pay cost of treatment, transport and communication difficulties, unqualified medical practitioners, and health centres are under staffed. Doctors and paramedical workers do not want to work in rural areas because of professional, personal and social reasons. Therefore, to remove such problem, enhancing number of primary health centres and the sub-centres is not only solution, rather to develop philosophy of providing integrated health care system. For making health service more meaningful to people of the country, it is necessary to bring about fundamental change in focus and approach to entire health care delivery system in general and above rural health services in particular.

Divya Shukla (2008) in her study 'Rural women and their Nutritional Health' finds women are over-represented among poor. Poverty is associated with higher female employment but lower income, with great drudgery in domestic work but lower access to support services and with high fertility. All these contribute to poorer nutrition and health status of families.

B.V. Sandhyavani (2008) in her study 'health problem of Rural Women' emphasises rural people in India in general and tribe in particular have their own beliefs and practices regarding health. Some still believe in taboos, witch culture, some seek remedies through magical-religious practice and some opt for undocumented traditional medicine in addition to *Ayurveda, Unani, Siddha* and *Naturopathy*. Basic nature of health problem is attributing to health literature and health consciousness, poor maternal and child health services and occupational hazards.

Universe of the Study

Universe of the study is selected tea estates in Cachar district of Assam and the district is consisted more than two dozen large and small tea estates. Although the Health Ministries of both Central and State Governments spend a lot in health sector, still we can sharply observe the worse health and traditional health care practices in the tea estates of the district. The inhabitants of tea gardens are very poor and most of them face many health related problems. According to 2011 Census, total population of Assam is 31,169,272 and total population of Cachar is 1,736,391. The district is heterogeneous in character consist of plain tribe, hill tribes and non-tribal add specialty for study of health problems. Non-tribal people are in majority in descending order—Hindu, Muslim and Christian as well. In the valley, many health centres, both public and private, exist providing enough scope to study. For this purposive study, the name of selected tea-estates is Rosekandi, T.E., Darbi, T.E., Tocklai, T.E., Dayapur, T.E., Aarkatipur, T.E., Borakhai, T.E., West Jalenga, T.E., and Binodnagar, T.E.

Operational Definition

Health Care Practice: Health Care is more than medical care. It embraces a multitude of services provided to individual or Community by health Personnel aiming at promotion, protection and restoration of the health services to its people through its Primary health care network. Health care practices vary from place to place and time to time. It is the prevalent system of curing disease with in a group of people in a regional setting.

Implication of the Study

The study may help a student of public health studies, teacher, researcher and planner in general to understand and analyses objective and state of health care practices and health policy programmer of government to spread health awareness among people of the valley and the state as well. Outcome of the study may also help planner for revising and reformulating health policy.

The Study Area

Cachar District: Cachar is an administrative district in the State of Assam in India. Silchar is district headquarters as well as one of the most business centre's of Assam and the only Lok Sabha Constituency of the district. It occupies an area of 3,786 square kilometres (1,462 sq. m.). The Barak is the main river of the district and a part from that there are numerous small rivers which flow from Dima Hasao district, Manipur or Mizoram. The district is mostly made-up of plains, but there are a number of hillocks spread throughout the district. These hillocks are very much useful for tea plantation. Apart from these many tea estates come to existence during British rule in India. Since then, the immigrants of Bihar, Odisha, and Madhya Pradesh occupy these tea estates. Moreover, the name of selected tea estates for this study purpose mentioned earlier.

Community

The study reveals that out of 320 households 271 (84.68%) families belong to Oriya community, 21 (6.57%) Bengali, 13 (4.06%) Muslim, 12 (3.75%) Khasi and 3 (0.93%) belongs to Manipuri community. Except the Muslim and Manipuri families, all others are followers of very low status in traditional Hindu society.

Occupation and Economy

Tea estates of Cachar district mainly occupied by the Bagani (Oriya based labourer) communities. Whereas, 96.1 per cent population of tea estates are directly engaged as daily wage worker and remaining are engaged with some other activities like cultivation, small business, *viz*. retailer of grocery items, carpentry etc. The villagers cultivate small land around their courtyard for kitchen purpose. Besides, they are conscious about plantation like betel nut, coconut tree, mango tree, guava, papaya and lemon tress etc. around their habitats. Labourers get their earning at the end of every week, i.e., Saturday evening. They earn nearly Rs. 500 per week while some permanent experienced workers draw more return from tea estate. As per collected data show 2 persons from 53.7 per cent families goes to the tea estate for works every day, whereas 3 persons from 13.5 per cent families, 4 persons from 6.3 per cent and 1 person from remaining 26.5 per cent families goes regularly. As per collected data, 94 per cent inhabitants of the study area live under below poverty line (BPL), whereas 6 per cent live above poverty line (APL). Only 4.8 per cent populations are covered by insurance policy (LIC and SBI Life Insurance Policy), whereas cent-per-cent of the villagers has ration card. Most (78.2%) of the families monthly income is 0-8000, 19.3 per cent have 8000-12000 and.5 per cent have 12000 and above. However, 63 per cent head of households have bank accounts either in UCO or in SBI and Assam Gramin Bikash Bank.

Education

From the study, it becomes clear that only a few people are able to touch college so far. In the study area, 47.9 per cent head of households are illiterate those who can't write even own name, whereas 26.3 per cent of them attained primary level, 19.1 per cent attained high school level, 5.2 per cent higher secondary level and 1.5 per cent attained college level. Whereas, Sarba Siksha

Abhijan Mission plays an important role under Right to Education Act concern to education of teen agers of the area.

Housing

In this study it is found that 74.8 per cent families live in *kachcha* houses which are either made of paper or straw and reeds etc., 17.4 per cent in semi-*pucca*, 6.5 per cent in *pucca* and remaining 1.3 per cent families in one storied buildings. All semi-*pucca* households benefited by the scheme "Indra Abash Jyojna". In the study area, 5 per cent people have their own land holdings. It is been found that maximum families have only one living room except kitchen while many of them have only one house on the courtyard and this accounts 57.3 per cent.

Transport and Communication

Though all selected tea estates are well connected by roadways but due to worsened condition these occupies front pages of local newspapers time-to-time. Moreover, six out of eight tea estates presently connected through gravel road under construction by Pradhan Mantri Gram Sadak Jojana.

In concern to telecommunication, these areas are lagging far behind where only 21.7 per cent families have mobile phone, 13.6 per cent have television, whereas 42.2 per cent have radio. Only 3.2 per cent household purchase newspaper regularly. Mainly they read local Bengali newspaper, namely *Dainik Prantajyoti*, *Dainik Jogasanka* and *Samoyik Prasanga*. After talking with house-heads of the study area, I come to know that they have little interest in politics and they are largely ignored by the political parties throughout the seasons except during election time.

Water and Electricity Supply

The study reveals that 42.7 per cent families of the study area benefited directly from the water supply scheme while 7.1 per cent benefited indirectly. Moreover, other families collect water from either pond or deep well available in the area. In concern to electricity supply only 24.3 per cent families are benefited. Whereas, under the Rajiv Gandhi Rural Electrification Scheme electrification is going on in the remote area.

Health Study

People living in the study area face insurmountable hardship. Health hazard is one of the alarming problems of them. They practice age-old health care to cure disease as their ancestor followed and it indicates that they are yet to know about modern health care *vis-à-vis* facility available to them. In the study area, malnutrition and anemic problems are common disease. Diseases like chronic abdomen, allergic reaction, breathing problem, chest pain, cardiac problem, dehydration, convulsions, stroke, blood vomiting and bleeding in pregnancy etc. are seen often among the inhabitants of the area. It is obvious that this kind of worsened and low status of health is seen due to poor quality of food consumption and hard labour.

Regarding health care, inhabitants prefers herbal and *ayurvedic* medicines than allopathic medicines. For any kind of chronic pain, i.e. body-ach, body swelling, and minor deformities they prefers to take home made medicines from *Bej* (*Kaviraj*) or *Tantric Baba*. The villagers usually organize community prayer in temples for *puja* purposes to satisfy their God and goddess to get rid of diseases. In study, it becomes apparent that 62.7 per cent families of the study area prefer herbal medicines, 10.1 per cent prefers *ayurvedic* whereas 27.2 per cent prefer contemporary Medicare practice. Almost two-thirds of the respondents are either smoker or drinker even though they perceived smoking and drinking as threat to health.

Many health awareness programmes held time-to-time that jointly organized by the "Mrityunjoy-108" ambulance service, Cachar and "Sarathi-104" helpline service provider with the help of National Rural Health Mission (NRHM), Assam. The goal of those programmes was to create health awareness among the villagers to take help from '108' and '104' helpline as well as vehicle service in any medical emergency. Beside these free immunization and polio vaccination programmes are organized frequently by the district health programmers.

Instead of this awareness campaign, the inhabitants of the study area are more conservative towards their traditional beliefs and ideas regarding birth control, maternity care etc. They usually deny for vasectomy and hesitate for contraception and using of copper-T and condoms. One of the reasons behind this is lack of awareness and poor economy too. In this study, out of 160 female respondents 26 women were pregnant whose period falls in between 0-28 weeks. Among these 26 women, 17 of them experienced as mother earlier. Out of 26 women, 12 regularly taking vaccine in appropriate time and six of them are irregular in this regard. Three have not registered their name in the Janani Suraksha and Vaccination Record Book of Maternity Welfare Scheme. Out of 26 women, 23 are suffering from either anemia or physical weakness and dizziness. Pregnant women of the study area usually avoid milk because they believe that it causes large babies and difficult birth. Some of them wear a red string around their abdomen to prevent infants to have a cleft or palate. They also believe that an infant may have characteristics of an object that the mother craves during pregnancy if the craving is not satisfied. New mothers are discouraged from taking showers for several days, and discouraged from getting out of bed for the first few hours after birth. Light foods are provided while meats, beans and bananas are avoided. Some women believe that breast-feeding less nutritious and hence they give cow and goat milk to the new born. Another important thing that is often visible among the females is use of '*Tabeez*' and threat on different parts of the body to cure dieases and get rid of ghost or devil. While this ritual is also popular among male persons of the village.

While now-a-day's sizeable number of population move for primary treatment to the nearest sub-centre and primary health centre located in or around the study area. Life expectancy of male population is less than female population and it is come to focus after getting information from the 31 widow respondents moreover, in comparison to the widow respondents information got from 18 widowers in this regard (for this figure the lower limit of age is set as 55 years).

Results

Outcomes indicated that misunderstanding, fear of death, fatalism, shame, preference for traditional healing, beliefs such as blood vomiting, breathing problem, blood pressure problem, and bleeding in pregnancy are contagious and other spiritual issues affected their decisions around accessing services. This finding provides important information for health providers who are involved in related service delivery.

Findings

All eight tea estates of the study area are facilitated with health centre which are run either by the tea management in their own cost or with collaboration with National Rural Health Mission (NRHM) as Public-Private Partnership (PPP) policy. However, with pen and paper management of these tea estates are showing the availability of doctors but in reality, there is no rural prescriptioner available for treatment. The sub-centres of the study area are availed with auxiliary nurse midwives (ANM), pharmacist, and peon. The health centres are also not well equipped for any kind of casualty purposes. These remain open during daytime only. Moreover, these are only one bedded sub-centre whereas a few numbers of medicine items, *viz*. painkiller, antibiotics, bronchodilators, and anti-anginals etc. are available.

Problems Faced during Data Collection/Field Visit

1. During daytime family heads as well as elder go to works. Hence, problem arises to collect data. While on every

Sunday (rest day), male workers usually take drinks and goes for playing play card so problem arises to meet them and to collect data.

2. Some female respondents being illiterate, they are non-cooperative to share some data related to health and family planning.
3. Some respondents did not like to disclose information regarding their earning, work hour, extra income and feedback of the tea estates.

Conclusion

Inhabitants of the study area do not get minimum requirements to be healthy. Hence, health conditions of people in tea-estates deteriorating very fast. The villagers do not have a holistic and integral concept of health, disease and treatment. The concept was shaped by their environmental factors, social condition and cultural beliefs. Health institution within the community centres on healer and non-trained midwife. Therefore, when somebody falls ill they first contact the *Baj* and *Dhai* to diagnoses causes of illness through divination, subsequently this leads to higher rates of death.

References

Basu, S.K. (1985), 'Health and Culture among the Under-Privileged Groups', *India in State of Health*, A. Mukherjee (ed.), Voluntary Health Association of India (VHAI), New Delhi.

Chandra, R.C. (1990), A *Population Geography,* New Delhi, Kalyani Press.

Channa, S.M. (1998), *Medical Anthropology: Health, Healers and Culture*, (ed.) Cosmo Publications.

Dak, T.M. (1997), *Sociology of Health in India*, (ed.) Rawat Publication, Jaipur.

Deodhar, N.S. (2001), *Health Situation in India*, 1st edn. New Delhi: Voluntary Health Association of India, 2001.

Kohli, A.S. and Sharma, S.R. (1997), *Organization of Social Welfare,* Anmol Publications Pvt. Ltd., New Delhi.

Mann, B.S. (1968), Family Planning among the Tribal's, in *Family Planning News*.

Misra, R.P. (1984), *Development Issues of Our Time*; Concept Publishing Company, New Delhi.

Mukhopadhyay, A., Srinivasan R., Bose A. *et al. Recommendations of Independent Commission on Health in India.* New Dehli: Voluntary Health Association of India, 2001.

National Academy of Science, (1986), *Population Growth and Economic Development Questions,* New Delhi, Kalyani Press.

Nitcher, Mark (1981), '*Towards a Culturally Responsive Health Care Delivery System in India*' (ed.) *Main Currents in Indian Sociology*, Vol. IV, New Delhi: Vikash Publishing Pvt. Ltd.

Subba, T.B. and Gosh, G.C. (2003), *The Anthropology of North-East India.* Orient Longman Pvt. Ltd., New Delhi.

Thomas J. Sullivan, (1998), *Introduction to Social Problems,* Allyn and Bacon, London.

9
Effect of Several Anthropometric, Bio-social and Lifestyle Variables on the Bengali Hindu Female

Breast Cancer Patients of the West Bengal, A Case-Control Study

Pushpita Purkayastha

Introduction

India is a sub-continent with wide ethnic, cultural, religious and economic diversity and variation in the health care infrastructure. The health care facility pattern is heterogeneous with numerous religions where the benefits of the awareness, early diagnosis and multidisciplinary treatment programmes have not reached. With rising incidence and awareness breast cancer is the commonest cancer in urban Indian females overtaking the uterine cervix cancer and the second commonest in rural Indian women. The numerous myths and ignorance that prevail in the Indian society result in an unrealistic fear of the disease. Women often do not present for medical care early enough due to various reasons such as illiteracy, lack of awareness and financial constrains. It is seen in majority of the breast cancer patients in India are still treated at locally advanced and metastatic stages. A multidisciplinary approach to breast cancer treatment is so vital is available only at a few selected regional centres. This review aims at providing a a few selected regional centres. This review aims at providing a correlation between several anthropometric, bio-social and lifestyle variables with the Bengali Hindu female breast cancer patients of the State West Bengal, India.

Breast cancer is a disease in which certain cells in the breast become abnormal and multiply without control or order to form a tumor. The most common form of breast cancer begins in cells lining the ducts that carry milk to the nipple (ductal cancer). Other forms of breast cancer begin in the glands that produce milk (lobular cancer) or in other parts of the breast. Breast cancer is the most commonly occurring cancer among women, and its incidence is increasing worldwide. Breast carcinoma (BC) is the most common malignancy among females worldwide and more than 1,000,000 new cases are diagnosed every year. Breast carcinoma may be early or late onset, depending on age at onset. However, the cut off value ranging from 35 to 50 years for early onset breast carcinoma varies among investigators[1]. Despite this discrepancy, younger women with breast carcinoma exhibit more aggressive pathological features, including larger tumor size, tumors of higher grade (grade III), presence of positive lymph nodes, absence of steroid receptors, and a high s-shaped fraction, than do older women with breast carcinoma[2]. The rate of DNA and RNA mutations can be too high under some conditions such as: unhealthy environment (due to radiation, chemicals, etc.), poor diet (unhealthy cell environment), people with genetic predispositions to mutations and people of advanced age (above 80)[1].

The breast is composed of two main types of tissues, i.e., glandular tissues and stromal (supporting) tissues. Glandular tissues house the milk-producing glands (lobules) and the ducts (the milk passages) while stromal tissues include fatty and fibrous connective tissues of the breast. The breast is also made up of lymphatic tissue-immune system tissue that removes cellular fluids and waste[1].

Risk Factors and Causes of Breast Cancer

Research is ongoing to identify the exact causes of breast cancer. Researchers have, however, identified several breast cancer risk factors. A risk factor is something that increases the chance that a person will develop a disease. It is not a guarantee and does not predict a future diagnosis. Risk factors for breast cancer include:

A Previous History of Breast Cancer: A woman who has had breast cancer has an increased risk of getting breast cancer in the other breast. People who have previously been diagnosed with breast, ovarian, uterine, or bowel cancer have a higher risk of developing breast cancer in the future. Mothers of children with soft-tissue sarcoma may have an increased risk of breast cancer.

Significant Family History: If several members of patient's family have particular types of cancer, patient may have an increased risk of developing breast cancer[3].

Genetic Causes: Family history has long been known to be a risk factor for breast cancer. Both maternal and paternal relatives are important. The risk is highest if the affected relative developed breast cancer at a young age, had cancer in both breasts, or if she is a close relative. First-degree relatives, (mother, sister, daughter) are most important in estimating risk. Second-degree relatives (grandmother, aunt) with breast cancer may also increase risk. Breast cancer in a male increases the risk for all his close female relatives. BRCA1 and BRCA2 are abnormal genes that, when inherited, markedly increase the risk of breast cancer to a lifetime risk estimated between 40 and 85 per cent. Women who have the BRCA1 gene tend to develop to breast cancer at an early age.[3,4]

Hormonal Causes: Alteration in hormonal level may precipitate breast cancer. It could be attended by starting and stopping of periods (Menstrual Cycle), pregnancy in early age, hormonal replacement therapy, use of oral pills etc. An early age at menarche, a short menstrual cycle length, and a high age at first full term pregnancy or nulliparity are well known risk factors for breast cancer. In a study in Sweden, menstrual cycle length has previously been reported to differ between breast cancer patients with and without a family history of breast cancer and also between breast cancer patients and controls.

Pregnancy, Childbearing and Breastfeeding: Lower age of first childbirth, compared to the average age of 24, having more children (about 7% lowered risk per child), and breastfeeding (4.3% per breastfeeding year, with an average relative risk around 0.7) have all been correlated to lowered breast cancer risk in large studies. Women who give birth and breast-feed by the age of 20 may have even greater protection. In contrast, for instance, having the first live birth after age 30 doubles the risk compared to having first live birth at age less than 25. Never having children triples the risk. However, the risks involved in having a child are significant[5].

Life Style and Dietary Cause: Sedentary life style, high dietary intake of fat, obesity particularly in post-menopausal women may cause breast cancer. The consumption of alcohol is also considered as another risk factor of breast cancer. The risk increases with the amount and duration of alcohol intake. Women who consume two to five alcoholic beverages per day have a risk of about one and a half times that of non-drinkers for the development of breast cancer. A study of more than one million middle-aged British women concluded that each daily alcoholic beverage increases the incidence of breast cancer by 11 cases per 1000 women. This means that among a group of 1000 women who have one drink per day, they will have 11 extra cases of breast cancer when compared to a group of women who drink less than one alcoholic beverage per week; a group of 1000 women who have four drinks per day will have an extra 44 cases of breast cancer compared to non-drinkers. One or two drinks each day increases the relative risk to 150 per cent of normal, and six drinks per day increases the risk to 330 per cent of normal. Approximately 6 per cent of breast cancers reported in the UK are due to women drinking alcohol[6].

Sign and Symptoms: The classical symptom for breast cancer is a lump found in the breast or armpit. Doing monthly breast self-exam (BSE) is a great way to be familiar with the breast's texture, cyclical changes, size, and skin condition. The general alerting features of breast cancer are such as swelling or lump (mass) in the breast, swelling in the armpit (lymph nodes), nipple discharge (clear or bloody), pain in the nipple, inverted (retracted) nipple, scaly or pitted skin on nipple, persistent tenderness of the breast, and unusual breast pain or discomfort. In advanced stage (Metastatic) of disease underarm lymph nodes are present with other symptoms such as bone pain (bone metastases), shortness of breath (lung metastases), drop in appetite (liver metastases), unintentional weight loss (liver metastases), headaches, neurological pain or weakness[7].

Obesity, Anthropometry and Breast Cancer

Over 20 years ago, de Waard (1975) reviewed the epidemiologic research on weight, height and breast cancer in search of clues about the role of nutrition in breast cancer etiology. He postulated that the underlying mechanisms would involve endogenous hormones and metabolism. Since that time, however, epidemiologic and experimental research on breast cancer has focused on specific dietary factors such as elevated fat intake, that might cause breast cancer (Harris *et al.*, 1992). Many studies have investigated the relationship between anthropometric characteristics, particularly height, weight, BMI, thorax size, waist size, hip circumference and WHR and breast cancer risk throughout a woman's life[8]. In other words it is argued that being overweight before the age of 18 years is associated with a reduced risk of breast cancer in pre-menopausal women, while being overweight after the age of 16 years is associated with a higher risk of post-menopausal but not of pre-menopausal breast cancer. Weight change that occurs at the time a woman is undergoing hormonal changes (i.e. puberty, pregnancy, menopause, has also been suggested to have an effect on risk[9]. Although various biological mechanisms by which weight may influence breast cancer risk have been proposed, of particular relevance is an increase in circulating endogenous sex hormones, particularly estrogen[10]. Collectively the evidence suggests that the efforts of body mass index (BMI) and of adult weight gain on the risk of breast cancer are dependent on menopausal status at diagnosis. There appears to be inverse relation between both BMI and weight and the risk of pre-menopausal breast cancer; whereas there is a positive association between body weight, BMI and adult weight gain on the risk of breast cancer after the menopause[9]. Birth weight and adult height have been associated with an increased risk of breast cancer in both menopausal strata[9].

A recent study from India indicated that increased body mass index, waist size and hip size were risk factors for breast cancer both in pre-and postmenopausal women[11]. However, a study of pre-menopausal Vietnamese and Chinese women found that BMI was not significantly related to breast cancer risk[12]. In addition, evidence from Iran suggests that lack of physical activity and sedentary life style are responsible for the emerging obesity[13], although the role of nutrition should not be neglected.

Materials and Methods

My study contains 150 female subjects out of which 50 cases are pre- and post-menopausal women with histologically confirmed cases of breast cancer and 100 healthy women as control. For the purpose of the study three hospitals had been selected from Kolkata Metropolitan city of the State of West Bengal. The hospitals selected were: (i) Netaji Subhas Chandra Cancer Research Institute, (ii) Calcutta National Medical College, and (iii) Cancer Centre Welfare Home and Research Institute. Apart from the hospitals the study was also conducted on the normal lives who are not the victims of breast cancer. Data of women previously diagnosed cancer were also taken. 100 controls were randomly selected from pre- and post-menopausal women while doing the study.

Breast cancer patients from the above mentioned hospitals were contacted with proper permission from authority of the respective hospitals. After that an interview for the patients was conducted with the help of the staff nurses of the respective hospitals. In the interview a pre-structured questionnaire for collecting data on relevant information on family history, reproductive and medical histories and selected life-style factors including history of alcohol intake, use oral contraceptives pills, dietary habit was given to each patient. Then I took thorax, waist and hip circumference of each patient with the help of registered nurses of the respective hospitals with proper prior consent from them. I also collected various data on socio-economic status like age, occupational category of the woman (profession/ administrator/executive) and marital status (ever married/never married/widowed/divorce) by visiting each and every patients house. Data on age at menarche was collected by asking the subjects to tell the dates of their first menstruation (to the nearest month, if not date). Few women were not able to recall their age of menarche. In that case, they were asked to recall the season or some festivals nearest to their onset of menstruation, so as to assess their age at menarche.

Data on general menstrual characters include regular and irregular periods, length of the menstrual cycle, and duration of menstrual flow. Here irregular period is defined as the menstruation that takes place at a non-specific interval of time; menstrual period; menstrual cycle length as the time difference between two successive menstrual periods. Information on peak discharge has been collected on the basis of subject reporting the frequency of changing the absorbents. Menopausal status was defined when there have been no menses for a year. To ensure that variable were as accurate as possible with regard to menopause, the whole set of answers on date and type of menopause (natural or induced by bilateral oophorectomy, chemotherapy, radiotherapy or other treatment) date of late menstruation, date of start of menopausal, symptoms and date of hysterectomy were taken into account. Post-menopause was defined as the cessation of periods for natural reasons or due to radiation, chemotherapy or surgery. The adjustment variables taken into account were, in first-degree relatives (yes/no), family history of cancer, age at diagnosis, number of issues, duration of breast feeding, lactation history, hysterectomy, previous use of oral contraceptive pills, symptoms, alcohol consumption (ever/never), smoking status (ever a regular smoker/non-smoker), diet history, physical activity, medical history and reproductive characteristics of breast cancer cases and controls were taken. The variables of interest like height and weight of the subjects were measured by anthropometric rod and weighing machine and variables like thorax, waist and hip circumferences were measured by steel tape. Thorax circumference, measured at the base of the breast, waist circumference at the narrowest torso circumference and hip circumference at the widest. Additional adjustments were made for BMI in specific analysis. Based on the BMI, women were grouped into different categories as recommended by the WHO: normal range (BMI = 18.5 – 24.9 kg/m^2), overweight (BMI = 25-29.9 kg/m^2), and obese (BMI ≥ 30 kg/m^2). For data on control subjects were those women who did not have any record of any hysterectomy and cancer in their family.

The statistical programme SPSS 7.5 version was used. Descriptive statistics include mean, standard deviation (SD), and frequency distribution. Inferential statistics includes chi-square and student *t*-test. Tests for trend were performed to calculate odds ratio and 95 per cent confidence intervals as measures of relative risk. The test calculates Chi-square for trend, the associated P-value and the odds ratio for each category compared with the reference category. T-test was carried out to compare the BMI, WHR, height, weight, thorax, waist and hip circumference mean differences between cases and controls.

In all, 50 breast cancer cases and 100 controls were studied. The characteristics of cases and controls are shown in Table 9.1. With regard to the family history of breast cancer in first or second degree relatives, there was a significant difference between cases and controls (P = 0.000000). Compared with those who involved in long sitting time job or low energy expenditure or sedentary

Results

Table 9.1: Demographic, medical history, and reproductive characteristics of breast cancer cases and controls

Variable	*Cases (n = 50)*	*Controls (n = 100)*	*Odds ratio (95% CI)*	*Test for trend*
Age (years)				
<50	30 (60)	51 (51)	1.1 (0.6-2.0)	
50-54	3 (6)	9 (9)	0.6 (0.1-2.5)	χ^2 = 2.0
55-59	5 (10)	17 (17)	0.5 (0.2-1.6)	P = 0.57
60>	12 (24)	23 (23)	1.0 (0.4-2.2)	
Mean (SD)	50.6 (11.8)	51.5 (9.2)		
Marital status				
Never married	1 (2)	3 (3)	0.6 (0.0-6.5)	
Married	44 (88)	87 (87)	1.0 (0.6-1.6)	χ^2 = 0.6
Widowed	5 (10)	9 (9)	1.1 (0.3-3.4)	P=0.88
Divorced	0	1 (1)	0 (0 to NAN)	
Family history of cancer				
None	33 (66)	100 (100)	0.6 (0.3-1.1)	χ^2 = 38.3
First or second degree	17 (34)	0	infinity (NAN to infinity)	P = 0.000000
Occupational types of the women				
Housewife	2 (4)	53 (53)	0.0 (0.0-0.3)	
Service	47 (94)	15 (15)	6.2 (3.1-12.2)	χ^2 = 25.6
Teaching	0	13 (13)	0 (0 to NAN)	P = 0.000000
Others	1 (2)	19 (19)	0.1 (0.0-0.8)	
Age at menarche				
<13	19 (38)	46 (46)	0.8 (0.4-1.5)	
13	17 (34)	18 (18)	1.8 (0.8-3.9)	χ^2 = 6.1
14	8 (16)	27 (27)	0.5 (0.2-1.3)	P = 0.10
14>	6 (12)	9 (9)	1.3 (0.4-3.9)	

(Contd.)

Table 9.1: (*Contd.*)

Variable	*Cases (n = 50)*	*Controls (n = 100)*	*Odds ratio (95% CI)*	*Test for trend*
Regularity of the menstrual periods				
Regular	40 (80)	84 (84)	0.9 (0.5-1.5)	$\chi^2 = 0.3$
Irregular	10 (20)	16 (16)	1.2 (0.5-2.9)	P = 0.54
Age at menopause (years)				
<45	28 (56)	41 (41)	1.3 (0.7-2.4)	
45-50	16 (32)	47 (47)	0.6 (0.3-1.3)	$\chi^2 = 3.4$
>50	6 (12)	12 (12)	1 (0.3-2.8)	P = 0.18
Post-menopause therapy				
Yes	10 (20)	13 (13)	1.5 (0.6-3.7)	
No	40 (80)	79 (79)	1.0 (0.6-1.6)	$\chi^2 = 5.0$
NA	0	8 (8)	0 (to NAN)	P = 0.07
Duration of the breastfeeding (last child)				
Less than 5 months	29 (58)	2 (2)	29 (6.6-126.4)	
6 months to 1 year	13 (26)	19 (19)	1.3 (0.6-2.9)	$\chi^2 = 74.1$
More than 1 year	8 (16)	79 (79)	0.2 (0.0-0.45)	P = 0.000000
Previous use of contraceptive pills				
None	21 (42)	81 (81)	0.5 (0.2-0.9)	
Yes	29 (58)	17 (17)	3.4 (1.7-6.7)	$\chi^2 = 26.7$
NA	0	2 (2)	0 (0 to NAN)	P = 0.000001
Alcohol consumption				
None	46 (92)	98 (98)	0.9 (0.5-1.5)	$\chi^2 = 3.1$
Yes	4 (8)	2 (2)	4 (0.7-22.5)	P = 0.07

Calculated by χ^2 tests.

Table 9.2: Comparison of various anthropometric characteristics between breast cancer cases and non-cases

Variable	*Cases Mean (S.D)* *(n = 50)*	*Controls Mean (S.D)* *(n = 100)*	*p-value*
Height	154.5 (5.4)	154.5 (5.4)	P = 0.11
Weight	54.9 (10.4)	56.2 (8.9)	P = 0.75
Body Mass Index	22.9 (3.9)	23.53 (4.0)	P = 0.81
Thorax circumference	92.4 (12.7)	91.9 (7.5)	P = 0.26
Hip circumference	94.8 (13.9)	94.6 (8.8)	P = 0.12
Waist hip ratio	0.9 (0.1)	0.8 (0.1)	P = 0.02

Calculated by *t*-tests

occupation, weight gain of greater than 10 pounds among women with high-activity jobs was significantly associated with an increase in the risk of breast cancer [odd ratio (OR) = 6.2; 95% confidence interval (CI) = 3.1–12.2]. Oral contraceptives had been used by more of the case than control subjects (P = 0.000001), and duration of breastfeeding was also positively related in the case than control subjects (P = 0.000000). There were no other statistically significant differences between the case and control subjects with respect to age at menarche, marital status, age at menopause, regularity of the menstrual periods and alcohol consumption (Table 9.1).

Table 9.2 compares the mean values for various anthropometric measures for the cases and controls as a whole. With regard to the BMI categories there was no significant difference between cases and controls (Table 9.2). Neither was there any significant difference in thorax, waist and hip circumference between cases and controls subjects. In addition, when the WHR mean difference between cases and controls was assessed, a significant difference was observed indicating that the mean WHR was slightly higher in cases as compared to controls (P = 0.02).

Discussion

The objectives of the present study are to study the various anthropometric and bio-social variables associated with breast cancer and to understand the influence of diet and other lifestyle variables on breast cancer.

I have found in my study that job involving long sitting time or low energy expenditure were related to increased incidence rates of cancer of the breast, although the SIR were reduced among women with high-activity jobs. These findings are in line with the observations from two earlier investigations in other populations[38,39], including a follow-up study among college alumnae[14]. By using death certificate data in Washington State, standardized proportionate mortality ratios were estimated for breast cancer in several occupational activity levels[15]. All the studies mentioned above like mine, suggested that physical activity may decrease the risk of breast cancer and certain cancers of the female reproductive system.

The increased incidence of female cancers among professionals, government officials and clerical workers might be related to other characteristics in addition to their sedentary occupation. Because women with these occupations are usually better educated, they are more likely to adopt Western life styles, such as a high intake of animal fat. Dietary fat, especially fat of animal origin, has been positively associated with the risks of cancer of the corpus uteri and ovary[16,17,18,19]], but its associated with breast cancer is still controversial[20]. At late age of first birth and low parity, the two major risk factors for these female cancers[16,17,21], may also affect my results because they may be related to socio-economic status. Unfortunately, I did not have data to adjust for the potential confounding effects of these factors.

Breastfeeding has been hypothesized to reduce the risk of breast cancer. However, early systematic reviews have not yielded consistent findings for the association between breast cancer risk and ever breastfeeding or cumulative breastfeeding duration[22-24]. Two out of the five case-control studies reported a significantly decreased risk of breast cancer for ever having breastfed when compared with never[25,26]. However, history of breastfeeding was limited to that for the last child in one[25] and parity or number of births was not considered as a confounding factor in the other[26]. Remaining three studies assessed the association of ever breastfeeding or duration of breastfeeding with the risk of breast cancer after considering number of births[27,28,29]. Yoo *et al.* [27] observed a non-significant, 38 per cent reduction of risk for ever having breastfed and the trend for decreasing risk with increasing duration of breastfeeding was statistically significant. About 40 per cent reduction of risk was observed among women who had breastfed for more than 25 months in a study reported by Yao-Hua *et al.*[29], this risk reduction was strongly significant to the present study. Overall, a protective effect of breastfeeding on breast cancer risk was suggested in some, but not all studies. History of breastfeeding is closely related to other aspects of births, including number of births and age at first birth.[30]

Besides cumulative duration of breastfeeding, characterization of breastfeeding such as initiation of breastfeeding, number of children breastfed, quantification of mixed feeding and reasons for cessation for breastfeeding would be expected for future studies.

Family history and oral contraceptive users are an important indicator of a woman's future risk of developing breast cancer[31,32,33], but not all reports agree[34,35]. Young women with BRCA1 or BRCA2 mutations who have used oral contraceptives may have an increased risk of breast cancer[35]; the same may be true for young woman with a family history of breast cancer[36]. However, a higher risk of pregnancy-associated breast cancer in BRCA1 and BRCA2 mutation carriers was also recently reported[37].

My study did not indicate significant associations between age at menarche, marital status, age at menopause, regularity of the menstrual periods and alcohol consumption and breast cancer. Height, weight, BMI, thorax circumference, waist and hip circumference were not related to breast cancer risk[11,12], whereas WHR was positively related to breast cancer risk, in agreement with other studies[38,39]. The decrease in risk observed with increasing WHR is in disagreement with past studies and reviews[38,39,40], which found a possible increase in risk of pre-menopausal breast cancer with increasing WHR. A high WHR, indicating an android body shape, is commonly related to abdominal obesity[41,42] and to certain hormonal specificities which increase breast cancer risk: (i) Hyperinsulinemia, an increase in Insulin-like growth factor I (IGF-I) activity resulting in a decrease in Sex Hormone Binding Globulin (SHBG) level[43], and (ii) higher levels of free oestrogen and testosterone due to a lower SHBG concentration[44,45].

Conclusion

This study confirmed that family history of breast cancer, occupational types, duration of the breastfeeding, oral contraceptive users and WHR were positively associated with breast cancer risk.

Having healthy food and regular exercises, avoiding tobacco and alcohol, avoiding hormone based medicines, avoiding direct sunlight and harmful radiations, following the breast self-examination, being slim and avoiding obesity should be done to say away from the pain and complication of the breast cancer. Glowing and soft skin, long and straight hairs, deep eyes, pink and rosy lips, ultra slim physique etc. does not mean the complete beauty. A woman has to be healthy too. Staying healthy does not mean only to stay disease free but it also means to be aware of warning symptoms of all diseases. Prevention is always better than cure and this way the women can take care and preserve their beauty that is God gifted.

Acknowledgements: I would like to thank all the people who talked to me about their experiences of living with breast cancer. Their comments and contributions were generous, full of insight and extremely valuable—both for this paper and for my own understanding, as someone who also lives with breast cancer.

I would like to thank my sir, Dr. Narendra Singh, Head, Department of Anthropology, Assam University: Diphu Campus, it was because of his unstinted and affectionate guidance that this work could see the light of the day. Last but not the least, I would like to thank my parents and also those who are instrumental, directly or indirectly, in the completion of this task. I thank all of them with a deep sense of gratitude.

References

1. What you need to know about breast cancer. National Cancer Institute. http://cancer.gov/cancertopics/wyntk/breast. Accessed March 13, 2013.
2. GLOBOCAN 2002, IARC [http://www.sunmed.org/incidence.html].
3. Eberl, M.M., Sunga, A.Y., Farrell, C.D., Mahoney, M.C. Patients with a Family History of Cancer: Identification and Management *JABFM*. 2005; 18:211-217.
4. Streuwing, J.P., Hartge, P., Wacholder, S., Baker, S.M., Berlin, M., McAdams, M., *et al.*: The risk of cancer associated with specific mutations of BRCA1 and BRCA2 among Ashkenazi jews. *N. Engl J. Med.*, 336(20): 1401-1408, 1997.
5. Newcomb, P.A., Storer, B.E., Longnecker, M.P., Mittendorf, R., Greenberg, E.R., Clapp, R.W., Burke, K.P., Willett, W.C., MacMahon, B. (1994-01-13). "Lactation and a reduced risk of premenopausal breast cancer". *New England Journal of Medicine* 330 (2): 81–87. doi:10.1056/NEJM199401133300201. PMID 8259187.
6. Allen, N.E., Beral, V., Casabonne D., *et al.* (March 2009). "Moderate alcohol intake and cancer incidence in women". *Journal of the National Cancer Institute,* 101 (5): 296–305. doi:10.1093/jnci/djn514. PMID 19244173.
7. Stephan, P., What you need to know about breast cancer symptoms. About.com: Breastcancer.06Dec2007).http://breastcancer.about.com/od/whatisbreastcancer/a/bc_symptoms.htm (20 Mar 2010).
8. van den Brandt, P.A., Spiegelman, D., Yaun, S.S., Adami, H.O., Beeson, L., Folsom, A.R. *et al*. Pooled analysis of prospective cohort studies on height, weight, and breast cancer risk. *Am J Epidemiol,* 2000; 152: 514-527.
9. Hung Z., Hankinson, S.E., Coldditz, G.A., Stampfer, M.J., Hunter, D.J., Manson, J.E., Hennekens, C.H., Rosner, B., Speiser, F.E., Willett, W.C.: Dual effects of weight and weight gain on breast cancer risk. JAMA, 1997, 278:1407-1411.
10. Bernstein, L., Ross, R.K.: Endogenous hormones and breast cancer risk. *Epidemiol Rev,* 1993, 15:48-65.
11. Mathew, A., Gajalakshmi, V., Rajan, B., Kanimozhi, V., Brennan, P., Mathew, B.S., Boffetta, P.: Anthropometric factors and breast cancer risk among urban and rural women in South India: a multicentric case-control study. *Br J Cancer,* 2008, 99: 207-213.

12. Nichols, H.B., Trentham-Dietz, A., Love, R.R., Hampton, J.M., Hoangann, P.T., Allred, D.C., Mohsin, S.K., Newcomb, P.A.: Differences in breast cancer risk factors by tumor marker sub-types among pre-menopausal Vietnamese and Chinese women. *Cancer Epidemiol Biomarkers Prev* 2005, 14:41-47.
13. Kelishadi, R., Alikhani, S., Delavari, A., Alaedini, F., Safaie, A., Hojatzadeh, E.: Obesity and associated lifestyle behaviours in Iran: findings from the first National Non-communicable Disease Risk Factor Surveillance Survey. *Public Health Nurt.*, 2008, 11: 246-251.
14. Frisch, R.E., Wyshak, G., Albright, N.L., Albright, T.E., Schiff, I., Wischi, J., *et al.* Lower lifetime occurrence of breast cancer and cancers of the reproductive system among former college athletes. *A m J Cliri Nutr.*, 1987; 45:328-35.
15. Vena, J.E., Graham, S., Zielezny, M., Brasure J., Swanson, M.K. Occupational exercise and risk of cancer. An *Clin. Nutr.,* 1987; 45: 1318-27.
16. Parazzini, F., La Vecchia, C., Boccholone, L., Franceschi, S. The epidemiology of endometrial cancer. *GynecoI Oncol.*, 1991; 41: l-16.
17. Parazzini, F., Franceschi, S., La Vecchia, C., Fasoli, M. The epidemiology of ovarian cancer. *Gynecol Oncol.*, 1991; 43:9-23.
18. Shu, X.O. Gao, Y.T., Yuan, J.M., Ziegler, R.G., Brinton, L.A. Dietary factors and epithelial ovarian cancer. *Br Cancer,* 1989; 59: 92-96.
19. Shu, X.O., Zheng, W., Potischman, N., Brinton, L.A., Hatch, M., Gao, Y.T., *et al.,* A population based case-control study of dietary factors and endometrial cancer in Shanghai. Atn J. *Epidemiol,* 1993; 137~155-6.
20. Willett, W. The search for the cause of breast and colon cancer. *Nature*, 1988; 338: 389-94.
21. Shu, X.O., Brinton, L.A., Zheng, W., Gao, Y.T., Jin, F., Fraurneni, J.F. Jr. A population-based case-control study of endometrial cancer in Shanghai, China. *Intl Cancer*, 1991; 49:38-43.
22. Newcomb, P.A. Lactation and breast cancer risk. *J. Mammary Gland BiolNeoplasia*, 1997; 2:311–8.
23. Lipworth, L., Bailey, L.R., Trichopoulos, D. History of breast-feeding in relation to breast cancer risk: a review of the epidemiologic literature. *J Natl Cancer Inst.,* 2000; 92:302–12.
24. Yang, L, Jacobsen, KH. A systematic review of the association between breastfeeding and breast cancer. *J Womens Health,* 2008; 17:1635–45.

25. Minami, Y., Ohuchi, N., Fukao, A., Hisamichi, S. Risk factors for breast cancer: a case-control study of screen-detected breast cancer in Miyagi Prefecture, Japan. *Breast Cancer Res Tre,at* 1997; 44:225-3.
26. Saeki, T., Sano, M., Komoike, Y., Sonoo, H., Honjyo, H., Ochiai, K., *et al.* No increase of breast cancer incidence in Japanese women who received hormone replacement therapy: overview of a case-control study of breast cancer risk in Japan. *Int J Clin Oncol.,* 2008; 13:8–11.
27. Yoo, K.Y., Tajima, K., Kuroishi, T., Hirose, K., Yoshida, M., Miura, S., *et al.*, Independent protective effect of lactation against breast cancer: a case-control study in Japan. *Am J Epidemiol,* 1992; 135: 726–33.
28. Wakai, K., Ohno, Y., Watanabe, S., Sakamoto, G., Kasumi, F., Suzuki, S., *et al.* Risk factors for breast cancer among Japanese women in Tokyo: a case-control study. *J Epidemiol,* 1994; 4:65–71.
29. Yao-Hua, H., Nagata, C., Shimizu, H., Kaneda, N., Kashiki, Y. Association of body mass index, physical activity, and reproductive histories with breast cancer: a case-control study in Gifu, Japan. *Breast Cancer Res Treat,* 1997; 43: 65–72.
30. Kawai, M., Minani, Y., Kuriyama, S., Kakizaki, M., Kakugawa, Y., Nishino, Y., *et al*. Reproductive factors, exogenous female hormone use and breast cancer risk in Japanese: the Miyagi cohort study. *Cancer Causes Control*, 2010; 21:135–45.
31. Magnusson C., Colditz G., Rosner B., Bergnstrom R., Persson I.: Association of family history and risk factors with breast cancer risk. *Cancer Causes Control*, 9 (3): 259-267, 1998.
32. Sattin, R.W., Rubin, G.L., Webster, L.A., Huezo, C.M., Wingo, P.A., Ory HW, *et al.*: Familial history and the risk of breast cancer. *JAMA*, 253 (13): 1908-1913, 1985.
33. Dupont, W.D., Page, D.L.: Breast cancer risk associated with proliferative disease, age at first birth, and a family history of breast cancer. *Am J Epidemiol*, 125(5): 769-779, 1987.
34. Sellers, T.A., Kushi, L.H., Potter, J.D., Kaye, S.A., Nelson, C.L., McGovern, P.G., *et al.*: Effects of family history, body-fat distribution, and reproductive factors on the risk of postmenopausal breast cancer. *N Engl J Med*, 326(20): 1323-1329, 1992.
35. Ma, H., Bernstein, L., Pike, M.C., Ursin, G. Reproductive factors and breast cancer risk according to joint estrogen and progesterone receptor status: a meta-analysis of epidemiological studies. *Breast Cancer Res.*, 2006; 8:R43.

36. Althuis, M.D., Fergenbaum, J.H., Garcia-Closas, M., Brinton, L.A., Madigan, M.P., Sherman, M.E. Etiology of hormone receptor-defined breast cancer: a systematic review of the literature. *Cancer Epidemiol Biomarkers Prev,* 2004; 13: 1558–68.
37. Kotsopoulos, J., Lubinski, J., Lynch, H.T., *et al*. Age at menarche and the risk of breast cancer in BRCA1 and BRCA2 mutation carriers. *Cancer Causes Control*, 2005; 16: 667–74.
38. Shu, X.O., Jin, F., Dai, Q., Rong, Shi, J., Potter, J.D., Brinton, L.A. *et al*. Association of body size and fat distribution with risk of breast cancer among Chinese women. *Int J Cancer,* 2001; 94 (3): 449-455.
39. Friedenreich, C.M., Courneya, K.S., Bryant, H.E.. Case-control study of anthropometric measures and breast cancer risk. *Int J Cancer,* 2002; 99 (3): 445-452.
40. Connolly, B.S., Barnett, C., Vogt, K.N., Li, T., Stone, J., Boyd, N.F. A meta-analysis of published literature on waist-to-hip ratio and risk of breast cancer. *Nutr Cancer*, 2002; 44 (2): 127-138.
41. Kaaks, R. Nutrition, hormones, and breast cancer: is insulin the missing link? *Cancer Causes Control*, 1996; 7: 605-625.
42. Kaaks, R., Lundin, E., Rinaldi, S., Manjer, J., Biessy, C., Soderberg, S. *et al*. Prospective study of IGF-I, IGF-binding proteins, and breast cancer risk, in northern and southern Sweden. *Cancer Causes Control*, 2002; 13 (4): 307-316.
43. Kalme, T., Koistinen, H., Loukovaara, M., Koistinen, R., Leinonen, P. Comparative studies on the regulation of insulin-like growth factor-binding protein-I (IGFBP-1) and sex hormone-binding globulin (SHBG) production by insulin and insulin-like growth factors in human hepatoma cells. *J Steroid Biochen Mol Biol*, 2003; 86: 197-200.
44. De, Ridder, C.M., Bruning, P.F., Zonderland, M.L., Thijssen, J.H., Blankenstein, M.A., Huisveld, I.A. *et al*. Body fat mass, body fat distribution, and plasma hormones in early puberty in females. *J Clin Endocrinol Metab,* 1990; 70 (4): 888-893.
45. Key, T.J., Appleby, P.N., Reeves, G.K., Roddam, A., Dorgan, J.F., Longcope, C. *et al*. Body mass index, serum sex hormones, and breast cancer risk in post-menopausal women. *J Natl Cancer Inst.*, 2003; 95: 1218-1226.

SECTION 3 : DEVELOPMENT IN NORTH EAST INDIA

10
Sustainable Development and Tribal Youth of Assam

Kh. Narendra Singh

Introduction

Achieving inclusive growth is the biggest challenge for the people of North East India to bring them into the mainstream. The best way to achieve inclusive growth is through developing people's skills, for which a multifaceted approach towards education and skills development is necessary to achieve growth. Assam is one of the unique States of North East India having different cultures, traditions and ethnic groups living together. According to 2001 Census the total population of Assam was 26,655,528. Of them, 3,308,570 persons are Scheduled Tribes (STs), constituting 12.4 per cent of the total population of the state. The state has registered 15.1 per cent decadal growth of ST population in 1991-2001. There are total twenty-three (23) notified STs in the state.

Scheduled Tribes and their Distribution in Assam

Among STs, Boro represents nearly half of the total ST population of the state (40.9%). Miri (17.8%), Mikir (10.7%), Rabha (8.4%), Kachari (i.e. Sonowal Kachari) (7.1%), and Lalung (5.2%) are the other major STs each having 5 per cent or above of total STs. Along with Boro they constitute 90 per cent ST population of the state. Besides them, Dimasa constitutes 3.4 per cent and Deori 1.2 per cent of the total ST population of the state. The ST population in Assam is predominantly rural with 95.3 per cent rural and only 4.7 per cent urban population. Of the eight major STs, Dimasa have recorded the highest 10.4 per cent urban population, followed by Mikir (8.3%). On the other hand Miri have recorded the lowest 1.8 per cent urban population (*Source*: Office of the Registrar General, India). The overall sex ratio of ST population is 972, which is below the national average for STs (978). Of the eight major STs, Lalung have recorded the highest sex ratio of 985, while it is the lowest among Dimasa (951). The state has recorded child sex ratio (0-6 age group) of 962, which is again lower than the national average (973) for STs.

Literacy among the Scheduled Tribes

The ST population of Assam has recorded 62.5 per cent literacy rate, which is well above the national average for STs (47.1%). The male and female literacy rate of 72.3 per cent and 52.4 per cent respectively show that women are lagging behind by 19.9 per cent. Kachari (Sonowal) with 81.4 per cent literacy rate are well ahead of others. On the other hand it is low among Mikir (53.7%). Among Kachari (Sonowal), the female literacy rate of 74.4 per cent is quite close to male (88.2%). Gender gap in literacy among Miri, however, has been recorded to be the highest. With 71.4 per cent male and 48.3 per cent female literacy, the Miri women are lagging way behind by as much as 23.1 per cent points. The Scheduled Tribes of Assam are predominantly cultivators as 70.6 per cent of the total ST main workers have been recorded as cultivators, while merely 6.1 per cent as agricultural labourer. The ST population in Assam is predominantly rural with 95.3 per cent rural and only 4.7 per cent urban population. Of the eight major STs, Dimasa have recorded the highest 10.4 per cent urban population and Miri have recorded the lowest 1.8 per cent urban population.

Dima Hasao (formerly North Cachar Hills) and Karbi Anglong, the two autonomous hill districts of Assam are predominantly tribal housing two important STs of Assam—the Dimasa and Mikir (now recognized as Karbi). As per 2001 Census, the North Cachar Hills has got the highest 68.3 per cent ST population, followed by Karbi Anglong (55.7%). In absolute number Karbi Anglong is on top sharing 13.7 per cent of the total ST population of the state. Hailakandi, Karimganj, and Cachar districts have a negligible presence of ST population. (*Source*: Office of the Registrar General, India).

Table 10.1: Population Growth in Assam between 2001 to 2011

State		*Total*	*2011*		*2001*
			Urban	*Rural*	
Assam	Persons	31,169,272	4,388,756	26,780,516	26,655,528
	Males	15,954,927	2,265,188	13,689,739	13,777,037
	Females	15,214,345	2,123,568	13,090,777	12,878,491
	Population Growth	16.93%			18.85%

Source: http://www.census2011.co.in/states.php

Tribal Youth and Employment Opportunities

Poverty in Assam is predominantly a rural phenomenon with close to 90 per cent of the population being rural. Rural poverty is more than twice that of urban poverty. Urban poverty in Assam is much lower than all India urban poverty whereas rural poverty is at a similar level as all India. Whereas urban poverty decreased steadily rural poverty showed fluctuations with very little decrease over the years. The population growth in Assam also implied that there has hardly been any reduction in the absolute number of the poor over the years. The main reasons for poor performance in terms of rural poverty are the continuously declining real wages of non-skilled agricultural labour and increasing unemployment among the youth. Growth of the rural

Table 10.2: Current Daily Status (CDS) Unemployment Rates (per 1000) by sex in Assam and Northeastern states

State	1993-94				2004-05			
	Rural		Urban		Rural		Urban	
	Male	Female	Male	Female	Male	Female	Male	Female
Arunachal Pradesh	19	4	18	73	16	11	26	119
Assam	70	124	65	256	60	87	81	140
Manipur	10	22	50	31	19	11	55	81
Meghalaya	6	2	16	41	2	7	37	39
Mizoram	10	5	4	5	8	3	13	22
Nagaland	21	6	69	67	40	22	47	104
Sikkim	6	17	19	49	29	21	33	55
Tripura	34	104	82	215	122	374	189	589
All India	56	56	67	105	80	87	75	116

Sources: *NSSO (1997): Employment and Unemployment in India, 1993-94, 50th Round, Report No. 409.*
NSSO (2006): Employment and Unemployment Situation in India, 2004-05, 61st Round, Report No. 515.

Table 10.3: Percentage of Population below the Poverty Line and Per Capita Consumption Expenditure

State	Percentage of Population below the Poverty Line		Per Capita Consumption Expenditure (Rupees per month)	
	1993-94	1999-2000	1993-94	1999-2000
Arunachal Pradesh	39.35	33.47	343.75	672.31
Assam	40.86	36.09	280.42	473.42
Manipur	33.78	28.54	305.79	596.36
Meghalaya	37.92	33.87	390.00	639.13
Mizoram	25.66	19.47	472.59	935.53
Nagaland	37.25	32.67	454.48	1005.99
Sikkim	41.43	36.55	321.12	559.97
Tripura	39.01	34.44	367.43	589.50
All India	35.97	26.10	328.18	590.98

Source: NHDP, pp. 147, 164-166.

economy is, therefore, the key to poverty reduction in Assam. Incidence of rural poverty is the highest among agricultural labour and least among self-employed in non-agriculture. Urban poverty is the highest among casual labour. Large proportions of the rural poor belong to the agricultural labour and self-employed in agriculture groups. The self-employed in the non-agricultural section form the largest proportion of the urban poor. Incidence of poverty among SC/STs is higher than the general level of incidence. More than 40 per cent of the poor are SC/STs.

Assam's achievements, in health and education are mostly below or at par with all India levels. There is a considerable overlap in development activities by different layers of government. Gap between plan outlay and utilization exists possibly due to the inability in mobilizing resources to meet the matching fund requirements for centrally sponsored programmes.

The vocational training centres introduced by the Government and NGOs needs to functional to all tribal areas and enrollment fee to such training centres should given free or with minimum cost. Advance courses with adequate infrastructure needs to be developed for organizing such centres.

Several NGOs started vocational training centres with a plan to facilitate jobs for the tribal youths of the state. The Institute of Cultural and Rural Development, an NGO in association with Right Foundation and National Council for Vocational Training, recently opened a vocational training institute at Bongaigaon (Assam) which aimed at providing certificate courses on IT, Communicative English, and Personality Development. The courses are chosen from National Council for Vocational Training under the Union Human Resource Ministry. Tribal youths trained with such courses may get employment opportunity in towns and cities (especially in Guwahati which is becoming a metropolitan city soon) in Shopping Malls, Cyber Cafes, Restaurants and Tourism industry etc.

Action needs to be taken to increase the effectiveness of service delivery; to encourage decentralization for better accountability and governance; to improve quality of public service provision through innovative means; and to transfer expenditure authority to local bodies that are directly responsible and accountable to the local people. In order to achieve sustainable poverty reduction, there is a need to focus on asset formation through employment generation programmes. All the agricultural lands needs better irrigation facilities and water management in order to encourage the self-employed in agriculture to diversify their activities and increase their incomes. Encourage local community for active participation in decision making by strengthening the decentralization process through Panchayati Raj Institutions. Improve the social status of women through better access to education apart from improving health care services. Finally, the present observations are preliminary and thus have its limitations. There is an urgent need for research studies on tribal youth of the state as well as the region so that corrective measures may be taken for sustainable development.

References

Aggarwal, S.C. and J.K. Goyal, (2000), "Trends in Youth Unemployment in India: An Empirical Analysis", *The Indian Journal of Labour Economics*, Vol. 43, No. 4.

Das, S.T. 1993. *Tribal Development and Socio-Cultural Matrix*. Delhi: Kanishka Publishers Distributers.

Dubey, A., (2000), *Hunger and Poverty in North Eastern States, Implications for Food Security*, paper presented at the National Seminar on Food Security in India, CESS Hyderabad, March 25-27.

Gardner, K. and Lewis, D. 1996. *Anthropology, Development and the Post-Modern Challenge*. London: Pluto Press.

Mohan, G. and Stokke, K. 2000. *Participatory development and empowerment: the dangers of localism* in *Third world Quarterly*, 21(2), 247-268.

NSSO (2006): *Employment and Unemployment Situation in India, 2004-05*, 61st Round, Report No. 515.

Roy Burman, B.K. 1989a. Problems and Prospects of Tribal Development in North-East India in *Economic and Political Weekly*, Vol. 24, No. 13 (Apr. 1, 1989), pp. 693-697.

Roy, Burman, B.K. 1989b. Tribal Development in Perspectives in Singh, J.P. and N.N. Vyas edited *Tribal Development: Past Effort and New Challenges*. Udaipur: Himanshu Publications.

Saravanan, Velayutham. 2006. Economic Decline of Tribes in Tamil Nadu: 1947-2000 in Govinda Chandra Rath edited *Tribal Development in India*. New Delhi: Sage.

Sharma, S.L. 1989. Tribal Development: Perspectives and Issues in Singh, J.P. and N.N. Vyas edited *Tribal Development: Past Effort and New Challenges*. Udaipur: Himanshu Publications.

Singh, J.P. and N.N. Vyas (Edt.). 1989. *Tribal Development: Past Effort and New Challenges*.Udaipur: Himanshu Publications.

11
Development Issues Related to the Tribes of North East India

Borkiri Terang and *Sangwaiso Teronpi*

Introduction

India is a land of multifaceted culture and home of varied communities, and it represents one of the richest ethnographic pictures in the world. Within its large and varied population across the length and breadth of the country, we find the North East Region (NER) of India, with its diverse tribal communities and distinct ethnic and cultural identities. North East Region in India is one of the most isolated regions in the country. This region, in the context of India occupies a distinctive place primarily due to its geographical, historical, social, cultural, and political features. It comprises eight states, including Arunachal Pradesh, Assam, Manipur, Meghalaya, Mizoram, Nagaland, Tripura and Sikkim. The North East Region has over 200 of the 635 tribal communities (NERLP Report) in the country and the tribal population constitutes about one-fourth of the population of the region.

With a total population of 39 million (2001), the region accounts for about 3.8 per cent of India's total population; it covers 7.98 per cent of its total geographical area. The economy of the NE region is still pre-dominantly agrarian with the share of agriculture in total State Domestic Product (SDP) above the national average. It is ironic that the North East Region has a vast reserve of natural resources and huge potential and avenues for development, but even today remains one of the poorest and underdeveloped regions of the country. The region has better than average Human Development Indices but poverty and unemployment is widespread in rural and urban areas leading to many social, economic, political and cultural issues. The standing scenario of the North East Region is one of seclusion, exclusion, neglect, isolation and underdevelopment when compared to the rest of India.

Who are the Tribal?

Indian Scheduled Tribes are the group of tribal communities and was given the name Scheduled Tribes during the post-Independence period, under the rule of Constitution of India. The Constitution of India, Article 366(25) defines Scheduled Tribes as "such tribes or tribal communities or part of or groups within such tribes or tribal communities as are deemed under Article 342 to the Scheduled Tribes (STs) for the purposes of this Constitution". In the Article 342, procedure to be followed for specification of Scheduled Tribe is prescribed. Though, it does not contain the criterion for the specification of any community as Scheduled Tribe, however a well established criterion that is being followed are based on certain attributes such as, geographical isolation, backwardness, distinctive culture, language and religion, shyness of contact. Thus, the Constitution of India provides for both protection and development of these historically backward communities.

What is Development?

Development essentially is a dynamic process which transforms an economy and society from a relatively backward state to a more advanced state. The transition encompasses several dimensions such as, growth and productivity and income, structural change in the economy and society, institutional changes, changes in attitude and values of people and even in customs and social practices. In other words the process of change will qualify as development only if results into an improvement in the quality of life of the people in terms of better nutrition and health standard, greater opportunity to be educated and elimination of deprivation from participation in social and economic life (UNDP Report). Traditionally, "development" refers to the capacity of a national economy to generate and sustain an annual increase in its gross national product (GNP). But in the present context, development is 'conceived of as a multi-dimensional process involving major changes in social structures, popular attitudes and national institutions as well as the acceleration of economic growth, the reduction of inequality and eradication of absolute poverty.'

Comparative Analysis of Development in NER

Most of the North-Eastern states are late comers in the development process. Incidentally, coinciding with the reorganisation of Assam, the North Eastern Council (NEC) came into being in 1972. Thus, from the beginning of the fifth year plan we find three channels of action in respect of north-eastern states; the Central plan, the State plan and the North Eastern Council. Even a passing glance of the inter-state growth is enough to reveal the acute differences in the levels of development. At the very outset, since different states were in different stages of development, and initial conditions were different, the response of all the states was consequently unequal. Such development gap led to aspiration gap and the people affected takes turn to the rigid action for further isolation instead of assimilation, absorption and growth. It has been found that the major Indian states have wide divergence in terms of development due to the differences in growth rate. The states of NER are behind many major states, particularly western and southern zones, in terms of per capita income and the obverse of it is the percentage of people below the poverty line. It is also difficult to compare the hill states of NER with that of the other states, because here agriculture and even the secondary sector are limited for sheer infrastructure and ecological reasons. Various factors like insufficient devolution of funds, lack of public as well private investments, inadequate human development and others have contributed towards the failure of north eastern states to come up to the level of advanced states. Hence, there is no convergence of growth among the states of India even after six decades of Independence.

Development Constraints

The development backwardness of the north-eastern region is almost proverbial. At the time of Independence, the North East was one of the most prosperous regions in the whole of India. But more than six decades later, this has become one of the most troubled and backward regions in the country. All the states in this region are included in the special category for the purpose of concessional financial treatment by the Central Government. It is often alleged that the persistent backwardness of the region stands in great contrast to its development potential. The NER has therefore more issues to be addressed and challenges to face than any other regions of the country. These issues implicitly have Social, Political, Economic, Geographical connotations which can be considered to be the main areas of underdevelopment among the tribes of the States of NER but for the purpose of this paper we will be giving an inter-related analysis of the related issues.

Among the most important social problems the tribes of NER can be said to be *illiterate*, though the region does have a higher literacy (65.83%) rate than the rest of India (64.80%). The State of Mizoram has the highest literacy rate of 88.80 per cent in the NER. Literacy level and educational attainment are vital indicators of development in a society. But in the NER a high literacy rate has not translated into a meaningful and satisfactory development of human life skills. The education system has not been able to provide skills and abilities needed to excel and gain employment in different service sectors. As a result the employment opportunities and employable workforce is missing in the region thereby aggravating the problem of *unemployment* in the region. The disproportionate growth of the service sector has led to the NER being undeveloped. It is to be noted that most of the urban centres in the region are administrative centres where except for government jobs, there are no, or very less of other employment opportunities. One of the main reasons for the unemployment rate being high is that even today agriculture remains the mainstay of the people of NER and this is true of even the tribes, who largely follow the method of shifting cultivation. Due to underdevelopment of industry and service sector, there has not been much change in the main occupancy of the region in the last decades. The self-employed in agriculture thus constitute the bulk of the poor which directly leads to the problem of *poverty*. The poverty rate in the region is significantly higher than the national average with the human development indices showing poor record and the lack of development further aggravating the problem. As many as 7.90 million persons were living below the poverty line in the NER (2004-05) as against 280 million in India (HDR, 2003, UNDP). As per Planning Commission, Government of India, BPL population in NER is 19.1 per cent as against 27.5 per cent at all India level. Among the States, Sikkim (20.1%) has the highest poverty ratio and poverty is higher than all India level in both the urban and rural areas. Closely related to poverty is the problem of *lack of basic health facilities* among the tribes of NER. An impoverished health condition proves detrimental to development process, thus attainment of basic health facilities is equally important for capacity development. In the NER, health related issues like lack of medical specialist, along with high incidence of AIDS, cancer, malaria and other diseases, has resulted in overall low human development.

From the point of view of *infrastructure development* the principal problem in the region is the inadequacy of communication facilities. The real picture of backwardness of the region is to be found in its extremely backward infrastructure. Weak infrastructure and poor connectivity hinder the realisation of the various development projects and schemes. The region is grossly deficient of infrastructure to tap the available resources and push the economy forward. The NER is lacking in terms of infrastructure in areas such as roads, electricity, drinking water and health facilities. Transport infrastructure is of great importance in the region to strengthen its integration within itself, with the rest of the country and its neighbours though it can be seen that there is wide scale neglect and unwillingness to develop it accordingly. The banking infrastructure has received considerable expansion in terms of commercial and rural branches in the NER in the post-nationalisation period. Low credit-deposit ratio is an indicator of not only infrastructural weakness but also entrepreneurial underdevelopment leading to drain of fund from the region. The *lack of investments*, both public and private is directly linked with the *underdevelopment of the industrial sector* in the NER. Most of the states of NER are heavily dependent on Central Government's assistance. And as such they have not made much effort to develop their internal financial resources. The NER has an extremely narrow industrial base so far as large and medium scale industries are concerned. The major industries like oil and tea are mainly concentrated in the State of Assam alone, which has resulted in a skewed industrial expansion in the other states. Therefore, even if there is no shortage of funds from the Central Government, effective utilisation of public finances to develop the industrial sector should be taken with immediate effect. In addition to public investment, private investment and foreign direct investments (FDI) in the development and expansion of the industries is of the utmost importance.

Coming to the issue of *resources*, it is not the lack of natural resources but the effective and optimal utilisation of the natural resources and the full exploitation of the mineral resources. The resources of the NER are very rich and varied but require greater enterprise for development. From the point of view of medium and large industry the most promising resources are the forest wealth of the region and the substantial deposits of oil, coal and limestone which have not been fully exposed. The problem lies in the fact that the governments of the NER states in spite of having such vast deposits are too weak and incapable to utilise those resources in industrial expansion. Along the same line the hydro power generation potential in the NER is largely untapped where the power requirements and consumption is growing everyday but the power generation is by and large fairly low. Like any other region anywhere in the world, *environmental problems* are a major concern even in the NER. The dilemma is that of striking a balance between development, especially industrial, and preserving the traditional environmental practices and relations of the tribes. The tribes of the NER are primarily considered to be "eco-system people" because of their close relation with the environment. The traditional environmental practices of the tribes like shifting cultivation has led to problems like deforestation, soil erosion, loss of soil fertility and others, which apart from damaging the prospect of forestry-based industrialisation but also has posed great threat to the fragile ecology and the very survival and dependency of the tribes of the region.

When the political scenario of the NER is usually mentioned, the issue that comes to the forefront is the working of the *governmental machinery* and the question of governance then assumes significant scrutiny in the light of development process. Government machinery in the States of NER is quite complicated in the light of problems such as corruption, squandering of public funds, deteriorating law and order, lack of transparency and accountability, bureaucratic rigmarole, insensitivity and so forth. The government of the States of NER do not follow a bottom up approach to development or decentralised and micro-level planning to garner a participatory development. The political crisis in the NER is integrally related with the *problem of identity*, which is an age old issue. The region is the home of extraordinarily diverse mosaic of ethnic groups having distinctive social, cultural and economic identity, more akin to their South Asia neighbours than most of India. This has led to many problems starting with identity movements, demands for autonomy in the shape of homeland/state/autonomous district councils, insurgency and such. Such demands are the result of the fear of political domination, economic negligence; cultural subjugation and geographical isolation from the rest of India. Sectarian strife and ethnic intolerance are detrimental to the very process of development and growth of the NER. Related intricately with the problem of identity is the concern of the erosion and withering away of *traditional political institutions and practices*. Many tribal societies were introduced to Western democratic systems by outside forces and without warning and this have contributed severely to the long existing political dilemma of whether to follow the newly introduced systems or adhere to the old customs and traditions. Following from the aforementioned political issues is the conception that the tribal groups have historically been *politically under-represented.* This has led to feelings of neglect, isolation, seclusion and underdevelopment in the region. Thus, the political class as well as the general public wants greater and better representation at the national level so that their region can be more accessible to greater opportunities.

General Strategy of Development

In order to address the development issues of the tribes of the North East Region (NER), the unique characteristics and needs of the tribes should be taken into consideration. The fragile development eco-system needs to be handled with the utmost discretion and care keeping in view the specific needs and interests of the region.

The education system should try to raise not only the literacy rate of the States of the NER but also aim at the all-round knowledge development and vocational training so that unemployment can be checked. Poverty can be adequately tackled with when the unemployed populace can be absorbed into the industries and other service sectors. The urban centres should also be transformed from urban administrative centres to urban commercial centres which would generate employment opportunities for the people. The region is richly endowed with bio-diversity, hydro-potential, minerals like oil and natural gas, coal, limestone, etc. and forest wealth. Thus, the government should try to develop the bountiful natural and mineral resources effectively and optimally. For this development, a strategy of joint public-private investments in the required areas should be adopted. The tribes consider the environment to be crucial and integral part of their daily lives. But over the years their practices have led to environmental degradation and losses which have threatened their fragile but harmonious coexistence. Thus, new and effective methods and alternatives, adopting the latest technologies and innovations should be used to preserve their dependency on the environment and also protect and preserve the environment itself. There has been consistent suggestion for dispersal of power through building institutions at the grassroots level for ensuring good governance. The bottom up approach, decentralisation of powers and micro-planning should be adopted with the utmost urgency. The spirit of adjustment and accommodation should be appropriately infused and awaken in the society for a wholesome development of the region.

Conclusion

Diversity is the key to understanding the tribal situation in North East India. Tribes in the region have diverse histories, cultures, languages, religions, social organizations, polities, economies and sizes. This point needs no substantiation. What needs attention are the directions towards which tribal societies of the region are orienting themselves. Numerous development initiatives were launched in the region after independence but they were not able to realise their intended objectives and potentialities.

What needs to be kept in mind is that the issue of development in NER is more of challenges than of opportunities. The issue of development in fact is holistic and inter-disciplinary in nature and, therefore, needs an understanding in an inclusive sense. It significantly requires assertion, both at the diagnostic and policy making-cum-implementation stages in the region. Hence, a serious review of development plans, programmes, policies, and priorities is needed before taking certain corrective measures to prevent the tribal societies of the region from falling into an abyss.

References

Catherine, Chopfoza, Tribal Development in India with Special Reference to Manipur: Trajectory and Literature, the *NEHU Journal*, Vol. VII, No. 1, 2009.

Dr. Banerjee, Amamlesh, Dr. Kar, Biman, *Economic Planning and Development of North Eastern States*.

Dr. Behera. M.C., *Globalisation and Development Dilemma, Reflections from North East India*.

Irshad Ali, A.N.M., Das, Indranoshee, *Tribal Situation of North East India*.

North East Rural Development Project, Social Assessment and Tribal Development Framework, Draft Final Report, May 2011, Ministry of Development of North Eastern Region (Government of India).

Report on Development of North Eastern Region, National Committee on the Development of Backward Areas, Planning Commission, Government of India, November 1981.

Singh, N. Bhupendro, *Globalization and North East India: Challenges and Opportunities*.

Subbal, Tanka, *Tribal Situations in India: Need for Review of Development Process*.

The Constitution of India and Scheduled Tribes.

The Scheduled Tribes and Scheduled Areas.

12
Poverty and Illiteracy in the Hill Districts of Manipur
Issues and Concerns

Thenkhogin Haokip

Introduction

Manipur is a hilly State, which lies on the North-Eastern border of India. It extends between 23°85′ and 25°86′ latitudes north and between 93°03′ and 94°78′ longitudes east. It covers an area of 23,327 square kilometres and is bounded on the north by Nagaland, on the west by Cachar of Assam, on the east by Burma (Myanmar) and on the south by Mizoram and Chin state of Burma. The territory which constitutes the present state of Manipur consists of a valley and a chain of hills which encircles the former on all sides. The hilly region covers about ninety-two per cent of the total geographical area of Manipur. The state is divided into nine administrative districts, *viz.*, Imphal West (capital), Imphal East, Thoubal, Bishnupur, Chandel, Churachandpur, Senapati, Tamenglong and Ukhrul. Hill areas refer to five hill districts, namely Chandel, Churachandpur, Senapati, Tamenglong and Ukhrul. "It is noteworthy that some tribal areas in the country are covered neither by the Fifth nor the Sixth Schedule of the Constitution. For instance, the hills of Manipur State which predominantly is tribal areas in demographic character". "Hill Areas" means such areas in the hill tracts of the Union Territory of Manipur as the Administrator may declare to be hill areas under the Manipur Land Revenue and Land Reforms Act, 1960 (Manipur Act 9 of 1966). There are 33 recognized different tribes living in the hill areas of Manipur.

The State of Manipur is inhabited by various ethnic communities having their own distinctive cultural affinity. These ethnic groups can be broadly divided into Meiteis, Naga Tirbes and Kuki-Chin-Mizo Tribes. There is also a sizeable number of Muslim population who are called Meitei Pangals. There are also the Scheduled Castes—Dhupi Dhobi, Lois, Muchi Ravidan, Namasudra, Patni, Sutradhar and Yaithibi. The hill areas of Manipur is inhabited by various tribal groups—Nagas and Kuki-Chin-Mizos. The Zeliangrong Nagas and few Kukis live in the Tamenglong District. The Maos, the Marams and the Thangals live in the Senapati blocks and the Kukis live in Sadar Hills blocks of Senapati District. The Tangkhuls and few Kukis live in the Ukhrul District. The Kukis, the Marings, the Mayons, the Mousangs, the Lamkangs and the Anals live in Chandel District. The Kuki-Chin-Mizo Tribes have their maximum concentration in and around Chandel and Churachandpur District. From time immemorial tribal communities constitute an important segment of Indian society.

In India, planned development at the national level started in true sense only after Independence. During the British rule, when the Indian economy as a whole was near stagnant the tribal areas were generally kept secluded and out of the normal process of administration and economic action. There was little infrastructure in the tribal areas excepting in a few pockets. The character of the tribal policy of the British government was isolation of tribal people from the rest of the population. Some of the British officers genuinely felt that left to themselves the tribal people would remain a happier lot. This was specifically true of the tribals in Manipur. Some welfare programmes and legislations were enacted and implemented by the British during the pre-independent period to mitigate the sufferings of the tribals and prevent their exploitation by the outsiders. However, there was no deliberate attempt to strengthen the economic base of these downtrodden backward communities in the country. It was only after the country became independent that the leaders began to talk in terms of planned economic and social development.. Analysis of backwardness of a country indicates that even in a relatively richer states, there are district which rank poorly on all indicators of human development. Similarly, in a poorer state there are districts with very high development indicators.

State of Poverty in the Hills of Manipur

Poverty is a state of deprivation. Traditionally, poverty is treated as a one-dimensional concept. For the sake of simplicity, it has been defined in terms of income only and highly linked with economic growth. Poverty is measured in different ways, predominantly in terms of inadequacy of income to procure a minimum level of calories intake. The concept of poverty in terms of income is interpreted as referring to a very minimum level of calories for the people to live, so that they do not die out of hunger, but not adequate to lead a human life with dignity. But the World Bank recognized, "Poverty is not only a problem of low incomes; rather, it is a multi-dimensional problem that includes low access to opportunities for developing human capital and to education...". The economy of the people of Manipur State is basically agrarian. About 70 per cent of the people in Manipur are engaged in agriculture for their livelihood. Number and percentage of population below poverty line for Manipur States, during 1999-2000 were 6.53 lakhs and 40.04 per cent respectively. In the hills for instance, the survey in Senapati District has reflected that farming and related work is the main occupation for about 92.9 per cent of Hindu workforce and 88.9 per cent Christian workforce.

As in the above observation, poverty in the hill areas of Manipur is not only about income poverty, but poverty beyond the income. The livelihood struggles coupled with the socioethnic tension rampant from time to time also contribute to the multidimensionality of poverty. Remoteness from towns and cities resulted in social isolation making it hard for the rural societies to access basic education, basic immunity and proper governance. However, the multidimensional poverty of the tribals in Manipur is neither inherited nor absent.

The preliterate tribal societies were self-sufficient with surplus produces which were bartered with other objects they could not make or produce of their own in their villages. Some tribals, especially the chiefs were rich with livestock and grain, gifted or taken from the villagers as tax. For instance, a traditional tribal Kuki village has a blacksmith, a priest (physician), a carpenter, craftsmen and the general people who were good farmers. They were satisfied beings, with daily activities of village life away from the knowledge of the fast expanding world of modernization and urbanization, that was about to steal their village-life contentment. This way, when modernization swept the surrounding valleys, the hill tribals' eyes of wants were opened to find themselves in great multidimensional poverty. Thus, they began to live with the attitude of being poor.

Since, colonial period, the land rights of the tribal people remains to be protected even to this day. For example, the Annual Administrative Report 2010-11, has cited the Gazettes of India, for considerable protection hill forest reserve area, tribal area protection and valley area reserves.

After the post-independent era, successive governments both at the Centre and State strive to uplift the tribals as other citizens in other parts of India through various developmental schemes like Employment Assurance Scheme (EAS), Integrated Rural Development Programme (IRDP), National Rural Employment Guarantee Scheme (NREGS) etc. These schemes except National Rural Employment Guarantee Scheme (NREGS) remained ineffective owing to wrong implementation strategies.

The tribal areas do not have proper communication system, business centres, educational institutions and many modern amenities for development and modernization. Neither the government nor any non-governmental organization care to put their efforts in these remote and outskirt places. Many of the offices to be opened at these places usually settles in the capital or the district headquarters. The chiefs or the chairman of the village were summon once in a blue moon, appeased and everything is done. The villagers had no idea of knowing what happens, how or when, while the official documents boast of the achievements of reaching these remote places. The relationship between the incidence of poverty and variables such as urbanization is also very significant. In urbanized villages, the rate of poverty is visibly decreasing. This is without a doubt, to the credit of the government schemes and development plans.

The actual incidences of poverty in the hills especially in the interior parts are on the alarming rate due to the people's attitude of being poor because they live in the remote villages. Crude methods of farming and traditional style of cultivating different variety of crops in a small field are also another factor for the poverty incidences in the remote villages. The use of Tucha, Champong (local name for small-size spade, *dao*) till date for cultivation testify this fact.

Lack of arable land has become very acute in recent years. Due to the practice of Jhuming and shifting cultivation, large areas of land had been consumed in jhuming and has reduced large area of land unfertile at least for next three or four years. This has made arable fertile land become scantier each year. Low productivity due to crude methods and equipment also rendered the tribals to poverty. Due to increase in population, and an increased in man's need, the number of people who depended on forest for their livelihood increases while the land available for cultivation remains the same, which lessens the products of the tribals year after year, leading them nearer towards the state of poverty.

One of the most important factors responsible for the incidents of poverty among the tribals is the lack of educational facilities which some authors term as educational poverty. For many decades developmental exercise could not achieve concrete results because most schools are not properly functional although schools exist in name. This has made the tribals backwards in most cases. In places where schools are functional, poverty has forces many young tribals to focus more on earning than learning.

The tribal constitutes only 8.2 per cent of the total population in India. So when nationwide reservation policy is made this percentage is generally followed. But different states follow their own reservation policy based on the need of their own states. In Manipur, the tribal population constitutes 40.17 per cent of the total population. So, when the state government tries to implement reservation policy based on the norm set by the Central Government, the job index of the plain Manipuris sore high and the tribal are left with very few jobs. This has ultimately made the tribal unhappy about the current job reservation in the state. This is one small example of the deprivation of opportunities to the tribals.

Educational Development in the Hills of Manipur

The American Baptist missionaries were the first to spread modern education in the hills, using the Roman script. Modern education in Manipur was started first by the colonial officers in the later part of 19th century. It was Major General N.E. Nuthall, who started the first Primary school in Manipur in the year 1872, followed by Sir James Johnstone in 1885.

It was Reverent and Mrs. W. Pettigrew who started a modern school in Ukhrul in 1896. The next year in 1987, there were about 21 students only. The State Government had earlier established a school three years ago at Mao Thana in 1893, but due to non-availability of students, the school was closed in 1932. These humble beginnings were the springs of the rivers of changes among the tribals. The traditional attitudes of suspicions and indifferences had kept the tribals from embracing the promises of modern education and its accompanying developments. It took many decades for the tribals to accept the developments through education and urbanization. Although, education was started in 1896, in one part of the hill area, the rest remain in the dark for decades without the light of modern education. The disparity in availability of educational facilities in one part of hill areas to another tells of this sad story. While education is almost a century old even in the hill areas, there are some villages which still do not enjoy the facilities of primary education in their villages in the interior parts. Devi (1989) reported that 110 Schools have been opened in the different school-less villages in the hill areas of Manipur. About a century after the introduction of modern education and six decades after independence, the issue of school-less villages still exists in the hill areas.

The Semantics of Literacy in the Hills of Manipur

The issue of literacy in hill areas is very different from what is being perceived through the literacy statistical reports. Many of them learn the alphabets as necessitated by their faith in Christianity where they need to read their Bible and songbooks which are in their dialects but use the English alphabets. For this reason, it is not surprising that many of these hill districts have higher literacy rates than both the national as well as the state literacy rate. There is nothing beyond these religious activities to their literacy. A literate person is expected to be aware of his surroundings through the print as well as visual media. Besides, the absence of these mediums, the village literates could not read beyond their religious books. Their literacy has nothing to help them in improving their living or making a new livelihood. In other word, they are technically illiterate in the secular term.

The word 'literate' as applied to the tribals is often understood as the ability to read and write their names. So, going by this definition, the literacy rate among tribal soars up. But in the absence of proper employment or government developmental schemes to absorb even the most literate person fails to contribute to the development of their economy. Instead, they remained confined to their traditional occupations in the village only as good as the completely illiterate ones themselves. Therefore, if productive and useful literacy is to be achieved, then appropriate education should be imparted to the interior tribals also. In order to achieve such goals the question of imparting tertiary or higher education adequately to the tribals in the hills of Manipur comes in the forefront. Vocational education and training to the younger tribal folks also will help them to improve their economy.

The next question related to the literacy of the tribals in Manipur is that, primary education had given them the ability to read, write and understand them too. But due to the lack of appropriate higher education, they could not nurture the talents of the young ones and finally ended up in the same agriculture field as their illiterate parents. In this case, one can see the disparity in the number of colleges between districts, between hills and valley. There are at present 73 colleges in Manipur affiliated to the Manipur University. Out of the total strength, only 17 colleges are located in the hill areas while the rest are concentrated in the valley. Another disparity in this regard is that one hill district has got only one college while there are about five colleges in another. Instances of such situation can be sited from the situation in Tamenglong district and Churachandpur district which have one and five colleges respectively.

Education in the post-modern era is no longer considered a privilege, instead is a birthright of every citizen in the civilized society. The great progress made by science and technology and the complexities of modern life have necessitated universal education of a reasonably good quality. However, to many tribals in the hill areas, education, especially Higher Education remained a privilege. The governments at the Centre as well as the State try to provide primary education to all. In any society, education is regarded as one of the most vital component of development. It must enable the individual to develop the activity and skill to earn a reasonable standard of living and it must also enable him to develop his creative faculties to the utmost so that intellectually, morally, physically and spiritually he is in a position to enrich his personality. But educational reform efforts without addressing socio-economic conditions are profoundly counter-productive.

According to the Census Report of 2011, the literacy rate at all India level is 74.00, while that of the State of Manipur is 79.80, which has rural literacy rate of 77.15 and urban literate of 85.98. This indicated that more than 20 per cent of the population remained illiterate both at the national as well as State level. The literacy rate of the hill districts of Manipur is shown as under:

Table 12.1: Literacy rates of hill districts in Manipur according to Census 2011

Sl. No.	*Districts*	*2011*	*2001*
1.	Chandel	70.85	56.20
2.	Churachandpur	84.29	70.60
3.	Senapati	75.00	59.80
4.	Tamenglong	70.40	59.30
5.	Ukhrul	81.87	73.10

Sources: Census Report of 2001 and 2011.

Education and Poverty in the Hills

Poverty has robbed the tribals of the opportunity for basic educational pursuits because of non-functionality of schools in the village, before the introduction of Right to Education Act 2009, which was implemented in Manipur from April 2010. Poverty has also robbed them of the desire and the zeal to pursue education because the need for food and clothing stand in the way ahead. Due to poverty, the tribal children find themselves in the school for few years only, before their labour force is required in the field. This way, the basic literacy (unproductive literacy) discussed above finds itself in abundance among the tribals. They had the notion that works in the villages do not require much intellectual learning. To them, a good strong able-worker was of more value than an educated fellow who couldn't work in their field. The best education to them was more knowledge of fieldworks, seed sowing, field selecting for growing particular grain, good farming, animal rearing etc. But as time passes by, the traditional methods of farming which were very unpredictable usually failed them. This reduces them to poverty when their fields do not yield enough for them to last the year. They could not avail the benefits of modern science and developments for their betterment due to mere ignorance and lack of education.

Poverty and illiteracy are reciprocal to each other in the sense that poverty hinders education so as illiteracy leads to poverty. This cycle will repeat unless education is made accessible to all. The basic relationship between poverty and education is, the greater the level of poverty the greater is the chance for illiteracy. Sometimes, even Non-Governmental Organizations or the Churches had to come to their rescue in deliberate cases of negligence from the appropriate authority. Thus, poverty of the households does not allow the tribals to make adequate investments in education; and low or zero levels of investment in education accentuate their poverty.

Concluding Remark

'The better late than never' type of educational awaking that recently swept the hills of Manipur is very significant. The hill people are now willing make sacrifices to earn education despite many difficulties. Formerly, poverty was a hindrance and an obstacle towards one's education but it is now rather seen as a challenge through education promising worthwhile future and something worth striving for in the general minds of the hill people. With this attitude, illiteracy can disappear very soon with the older generations, if balance development between the hills and the valley, between one district and another are emphasized and carried out with the same spirit and principle. The question of poverty can also be reduced to the minimum with balanced developmental and educational emphasis on all parts of the state. Unless education is made free or heavily subsidized, it cannot reach the under-privileged. When educational poverty is effectively addressed and contained, the question of multi-dimensional poverty will also subside to an extent. As long as educational poverty held its head high in the tribal society, the presence of poverty cannot be dismissed.

References

Catherine, C. (2009). Tribal Development in India with Special Reference to Manipur: Trajectory and Literature. *The NEHU Journal,* Vol. VII, No. 1, 67-88.

College Development Council, M.U. (2009). *College Statistics 2008-2009.* Imphal: Manipur University.

Devi, J. (1989). *Education in Manipur.* Imphal: Rai Pravina Brothers.

Forest, D.O. (2011). *Annual Administrative Report 2010-11.* Imphal: Department of Forest, GOM.

Natarajan, S. (1990). *Introduction to Economics of Education.* New Delhi: Sterling Publishers Pvt Ltd.

Nayyar, R. (1992). *Planning for Development of Backward Districts.* OUP.

Statistics, D.O. (2007). *Statistical Abstract Manipur.* Imphal: Directorate of Economics and Statistics.

Team, I.R. (December 2003). *Report on Impact of the Tribal Sub-Plan Implementation in Improving the Socio-Economic Condition of the Tribal People with Special Focus on Reduction of Poverty Level covering the States of Assam and Tamil Nadu.* New Delhi: The Planning Commission.

Tilak, J.B. (November 2005). *Post-Elementary Education, Poverty and Development in India.* Edinburgh: Centre of African Studies, University of Edinburgh.

TRI, M. (2008). *Annual Report 2007-08.* Imphal: Tribal Research Institute, Imphal.

University, M. (2010). *Annual Report 2009-10.* Imphal: Manipur University.

Zeliang, E. (2005). *History of Christianity in Manipur: Source Materials.* Imphal: CLC Guwahati.

Index